Great Retreats
for Youth Groups

YOUTH SPECIALTIES TITLES

Professional Resources
Advanced Peer Counseling in Youth Groups
The Church and the American Teenager (previously released as Growing Up in America)
Developing Spiritual Growth in Junior High Students
Feeding Your Forgotten Soul
Help! I'm a Volunteer Youth Worker!
High School Ministry
How to Recruit and Train Volunteer Youth Workers (previously released as Unsung Heroes)
Junior High Ministry (Revised Edition)
The Ministry of Nurture
Organizing Your Youth Ministry
Peer Counseling in Youth Groups
The Youth Minister's Survival Guide
Youth Ministry Nuts and Bolts

Discussion Starter Resources
Amazing Tension Getters
Get 'Em Talking
High School TalkSheets
Junior High TalkSheets
More High School TalkSheets
More Junior High TalkSheets
Option Plays
Parent Ministry TalkSheets
Tension Getters
Tension Getters Two

Special Needs and Issues
Divorce Recovery for Teenagers

Ideas Library
Ideas Combo 1-4, 5-8, 9-12, 13-16, 17-20, 21-24, 25-28, 29-32, 33-36, 37-40, 41-44, 45-48, 49-52, 53, 54
Ideas Index

Youth Ministry Programming
Adventure Games
Creative Bible Lessons
Creative Programming Ideas for Junior High Ministry
Creative Socials and Special Events
Good Clean Fun
Good Clean Fun, Volume 2
Great Fundraising Ideas for Youth Groups
Great Games for City Kids
Great Ideas for Small Youth Groups
Greatest Skits on Earth
Greatest Skits on Earth, Volume 2
Holiday Ideas for Youth Groups (Revised Edition)
Hot Illustrations for Youth Talks
Hot Talks
Junior High Game Nights
More Junior High Game Nights
On-Site: 40 On-Location Youth Programs
Play It! Great Games for Groups
Play It Again! More Great Games for Groups
Road Trip
Super Sketches for Youth Ministry
Teaching the Bible Creatively
Teaching the Truth About Sex
Up Close and Personal: How to Build Community in Your Youth Group

4th-6th Grade Ministry
Attention Grabbers for 4th-6th Graders
4th-6th Grade TalkSheets
Great Games for 4th-6th Graders
How to Survive Middle School
Incredible Stories
More Attention Grabbers for 4th-6th Graders
More Great Games for 4th-6th Graders
Quick and Easy Activities for 4th-6th Graders
More Quick and Easy Activities for 4th-6th Graders
Teach 'Toons

Clip Art
ArtSource Volume 1—Fantastic Activities
ArtSource Volume 2—Borders, Symbols, Holidays and Attention Getters
ArtSource Volume 3—Sports
ArtSource Volume 4—Phrases and Verses
ArtSource Volume 5—Amazing Oddities and Appalling Images
ArtSource Volume 6—Spiritual Topics
Youth Specialties Clip Art Book
Youth Specialties Clip Art Book, Volume 2
Youth Worker's Promo Kit
Youth Worker's Promo Kit Refill Pack #1

Video
Edge TV
God Views
Next Time I Fall in Love Video Curriculum
Promo Spots for Junior High Game Nights
Understanding Your Teenage Video Curriculum
Witnesses

Student Books
Going the Distance
Good Advice
Grow for It Journal
Grow for It Journal Through the Scriptures
How to Live with Your Parents Without Losing Your Mind
I Don't Remember Dropping the Skunk, But I Do Remember Trying to Breathe
Next Time I Fall in Love
Next Time I Fall in Love Journal

Great Retreats
for Youth Groups
12 complete faith-building weekends

Edited by
Chris Cannon

Youth
Specialties

Zondervan Publishing House

A Division of HarperCollins *Publishers*

Grand Rapids, Michigan

Great Retreats for Youth Groups
Copyright © 1994 by Youth Specialties, Inc.

Youth Specialties Books, 1224 Greenfield Drive, El Cajon, California 92021, are published by Zondervan Publishing House, 5300 Patterson, S.E., Grand Rapids, Michigan 49530.

Library of Congress Cataloging-in-Publication Data
Cannon, Chris
     Great retreats for youth groups: 12 complete faith-building weekends / Chris Cannon.
          p.   cm.
     ISBN 0-31-49161-4 (pbk.) : $12.95
     1. Retreats for youth. 2. Church work with youth. I. Title.
BV4447.C365   1994
269'.63—dc20

94-15086
CIP

Unless otherwise noted, all Scripture references are taken from the *Holy Bible: New International Version* (North American Edition), copyright © 1973, 1978, 1984 by the International Bible Society. Used by permission of Zondervan Bible Publishers.

Edited by Noel Becchetti and Lorraine Triggs
Design and typography by Rogers Design and Associates

Printed in the United States of America
94 95 96 97 98 99 / ML / 10 9 8 7 6 5 4 3 2 1

TABLE OF CONTENTS

ACKNOWLEDGEMENTS

Special thanks to:

- Cathy Dreger, whose ongoing support, prayers, assistance and encouragement have meant so much to me.
- Carl Dreizler, for lending a hand when I really needed it.
- Noel Becchetti, for believing in this project and in me.

Dedicated to:

- My parents, who paid for my first retreat.
- Stan Lazarian, who showed me the life-changing value of a great retreat.
- My wife, Anne, whose partnership, dedication and intuition have been invaluable to me (and for letting me go on so many retreats).
- And to the wonderful high schoolers at Hope Chapel who have given me the privilege of leading them on many memorable retreats.

DISCLAIMER

FOREWORD

ere's a great thought: "If we really wanted to be effective in Christian education, we would eliminate Sunday schools and use the money that we spent on them for camps and retreats. If you could get everyone in your church away for two weekend retreats a year, you would have more and better Christian education than a whole year's worth of one-hour Sunday school classes." John Westerhoff is probably right. There is absolutely nothing like getting away and focusing on God in a retreat setting. When you combine a good relational time with fun, learning, and extended time with God, you can't help but have a life-changing experience.

That's exactly what a retreat is all about. Many of us look back on retreats as some of the most significant spiritual times we have ever experienced. One mission organization says that seventy-five percent of their staff became Christians at a camp, conference, or retreat.

As we read between the lines in the Gospels, I believe that Jesus and his disciples had more than their share of retreats. Perhaps they had a rock-skimming contest on the sea of Galilee. Who knows—maybe Peter, James and John led the rest of the group in building a human pyramid during a three-day hike to Caperneum. I doubt if Jesus led a seminar on guy/girl relationships, but then again maybe he did, in his own way, as he and his followers camped by the Mount of Olives on one of their mission trips.

Chris Cannon has put together a practical, easy-to-follow, and extremely important, retreat book. Not only does my friend Chris know youth ministry like few else in America, he asked several of his friends to join him with their best topical retreat ideas. Chris knows youth ministry, he knows kids, and he definitely knows what works. I have often told people that Chris's ministry at Hope Chapel is one of the finest youth ministries I have ever seen.

As I have looked over the retreat programs and the authors, I can't help but believe you have in your hands a most valuable tool. What I like about the book is that these retreats aren't just ideas someone who does not know kids made up in his or her office. These retreats are proven *hands-on* events that have worked for some of America's finest youth workers. Now they put them in your hands.

My friend Wayne Rice taught me a long time ago that "the essence of creativity is the ability to copy!" Here's our chance to "copy" some great retreat ideas and, best of all, to see firsthand the spiritual fruit these events will generate in our own youth groups.

Thanks for your commitment to kids.

Jim Burns, President
National Institute of Youth Ministry

INTRODUCTION

Dr. John Perkins, founder of the Voice of Calvary Ministries and the Harambee Christian Center, recently stated: "I can do more with the kids in my ghetto in one weekend of camping than I can do in six months of contact work." Based on my ten years of experience in youth ministry at Hope Chapel in Hermosa Beach, California, I couldn't agree more with John Perkins' statement. Retreats impact kids' lives more than any other aspect of ministry. As I began putting together this book, I couldn't help but think back on some young people in our youth group:

Fritz came from a traditional Christian home and was a regular in our youth group, displaying the steady and consistent attendance youth pastors long for in their students. His best friend Rob used to be a regular too. But, unlike Fritz, who is now pursuing ministry as a full-time career, Rob seems to have lost interest, falling through the cracks as college interests have taken priority.

Cisco grew up in the barrio. He and his friend Dreamer were heavily involved in the same gang, living a life of crime. But, one day, only a few weeks after they came to a Tuesday night youth group meeting, both Cisco and Dreamer committed their lives to Christ. Tragically, Cisco was unmercifully gunned down in an ambush by fellow gang members who refused to let him turn from their group to follow Christ. Cisco literally died because of his strong faith in the Lord. Dreamer is now in jail, having returned to a life of crime.

Sherry recently left to serve as a missionary in Mexico. My wife and I couldn't believe we were saying farewell to the same person we had met many years ago as a timid, confused sophomore in our youth group. But there she was, at twenty-five, married with two beautiful little girls, about to embark on her own journey, serving others in a foreign country.

If you are involved in the lives of young people, you have your own stories. Some kids follow Christ from the day they meet him; others stray and return like the prodigal son; some drift from the faith, never to return. What makes the lives and spiritual journeys of Fritz, Cisco, and Sherry turn out differently than those of Rob and Dreamer? One common denominator of the first group is the fact that they went on weekend retreats. Their friends didn't.

Setting the Foundation

Not all kids who go on retreats become evangelists, missionaries and pastors. But retreats help set a foundation for, shape character within, and ignite a spark in kids that otherwise may not occur. Retreats can convert kids who watch from the perimeter of your youth group into men and women who are at the committed core of leadership and faith.

At a recent "This is Your Life" party my wife threw for my thirtieth birthday, I talked with Stan Lazarian, my Young Life leader who introduced me to Jesus Christ. As we talked, I was reminded of a weekend retreat that changed my life. It wasn't the typical surf or ski trip we take with some of our kids. Instead, it was a trip to Catalina Island, located about twenty-five miles off the coast of California. There my brother, a few other kids, and I spent the weekend restocking a Christian campground with canned food. It was grueling work, yet I discovered the joy of serving. I learned to skin dive. Dolphins jumped playfully around our boat. My brother got seasick and barfed his brains out. But most of all, I remember how much closer I grew to Christ during that experience.

What Makes Retreats Work?

There are many benefits to taking kids to unfamiliar surroundings. First, the new environment strips away roles they take on in their normal locales. The toughest guy or the snootiest girl can become more like other kids in the group. Second, retreats provide a "captive" audience for teaching purposes. The youth are away from the distractions of telephones, televisions, and portable CD players. Third, kids spend time with peers who can be more positive role models for them than many of their classmates at school. Fourth, kids at a retreat can experience a sense of community they have never known before. These factors combine to provide an arena where young people are open to the power of the Holy Spirit and to a closer relationship with God.

Retreats don't have to be complicated or require extensive travel. Nor do they have to be costly. There are places right in your own community where you can have overnight outings. Near our church there is an eleven-acre wildlife reserve set aside for overnight camping and day use. The cost per person is a hefty three dollars per day. We can also go to nearby botanical gardens, or simply spend the day whale-watching together.

It's All Here

This book has been written to help you to pull off life-changing retreats. It is designed so that you can duplicate and use the materials as they appear. Each retreat can be lifted right off the pages for your convenience. We've included all the necessary ingredients—including topical Bible studies, schedules, talk outlines, and lists of the materials you will need for each retreat.

I am thrilled to bring you these thirteen retreats (we've thrown in a "bonus" staff training weekend), tried and tested by their talented creators—seasoned youth pastors who have helped change the lives of thousands of young people around the country. They have done the work that could take the rest of us years to create from scratch. We all hope that you find this book a great tool to planning life-changing retreats for your kids. May God bless you and empower you as you help to advance his Kingdom through creative and thought-provoking retreats for the youth in your world.

Chris Cannon

SECTION ONE

A PRIMER
FOR
SUCCESSFUL RETREATS

Great Retreats for Youth Groups

Chapter One   *HOW TO USE THIS BOOK*

Have you ever noticed how many different ways a particular praise or worship song can be played or sung? We had just returned from a weekend retreat with several other youth groups. As we unloaded our van, I asked a girl in our youth group her impressions of the weekend. Her response was classic: "It was great, but it really bothered me that they played 'Humble Thyself' wrong."

This book is a little bit like that comment. Assembled here are thirteen retreats that have been tested and refined by their creators, who have passed their years of experience on to us. Yet each retreat is like a recipe. All the ingredients are supplied, but feel free to add a pinch of this or a pound of that. In some of the retreats, the authors will provide creative options. Use as much or as little of each retreat as you would like. Don't worry about plagiarism; the contributors would consider it an honor should you to steal any or all of the materials that are included. Also, no one will be offended if you drop or change any of the components given in a particular retreat! We want to facilitate the work you are doing by giving you retreat ideas that you can use as you like.

There are some things to keep in mind as you use this book. First, even though you have teaching outlines for each retreat, followed by an explanation of the key components, they're missing one thing: your personal touch. You will need to familiarize yourself enough with the material presented to be able to shape it to fit your group. Second, carefully and prayerfully consider where to have each retreat you organize. You'll want to consider various factors such as meeting space, sleeping capacity, bathrooms, kitchen facilities, and overall warmth. When using a location for the first time, a pre-visit is invaluable in determining the appropriateness of the site.

Finally, pray that God will bring the right people to your retreats. Chemistry, both spiritually and emotionally, is an integral part of any special time with young people and adult staff. Excluding interested kids from attending is *not* recommended, with the exception of specific retreats in which attendees have been a part of an application process (e.g., peer counseling, student leadership). Ask the Lord to bring the right people on your retreat.

It is a privilege to come alongside you as you endeavor to develop life-changing retreats that will produce greater depth and character in the lives of your high school and junior high students. May God bless you abundantly as you serve him!

Chapter Two

FIVE KEYS TO A MEMORABLE RETREAT

Memorable retreats are those where everyone feels comfortable, the settings are familiar, and challenges are kept to a minimum—right? Wrong. I've found five keys to be essential for memorable retreats:

Find unfamiliar settings or circumstances

When a retreat is held in a new location, or when new circumstances are introduced, adolescents find joy in exploring unseen territory. They can reach back to their days as children as they try something for the first time. In familiar surroundings, teenagers are often too caught up in the bumps and bruises of being adolescents. When they get away, however, each new experience creates a new memory. And because everyone is on new turf, a positive dependency on the group's leadership is often formed.

Create tension

Retreats are great settings for addressing the fears of adolescents. Often when a student is faced with a different experience, positive tension can result. Perhaps one student in your youth group is soft-spoken and not very popular. Try appointing him or her team captain for a game. Maybe another is afraid of hiking in the woods. Ask him or her to lead the group on a short walk from the cabins to a nearby location. Channeling this positive tension in creative ways can help teenagers experience the satisfaction of accomplishing something that previously seemed impossible. Retreats that create opportunities to overcome present fears can increase confidence for the future.

Present challenges

A setting minus the distractions of telephones, televisions, and other things that can divert attention provides an optimum learning environment for your kids. Make the most of it. Challenge students to pick up their Bibles during free time. Challenge them to focus on the teachings of the speaker. Challenge them to begin new friendships with people they didn't know before they left home.

Provide vehicles of encouragement

I remember taking an eye exam while applying for my Class Two Driver's License. At first, I was failing miserably. The nurse testing me was a real grouch. Thankfully, she was called away from the exam and another, friendlier nurse took over. With her encouragement, my score improved and I passed with flying colors. The most important task for a retreat leader is to give encouragement to every teenager present. Even if a boy or girl doesn't remember the theme of the retreat, the content of your talks, or the results of the games you played, one meaningful compliment or heart-to-heart talk may change his or her life forever.

Ensure that everyone gets plenty of rest

One of the most common faults in retreat planning is an overabundance of activities and events. While fast-paced schedules can be important to the success of your retreat, adequate rest is crucial. Fatigued minds will learn less and remember little. Here are two scheduling tips:

Designate the hour before dinner of the first full day of the retreat as "quiet time." This does not necessarily mean that everyone has to read their Bibles. Rather, designate it as a time when there is no talking. Encourage kids to sleep, go for a walk, pray, or do something else relaxing.

On the second night of the retreat, schedule "lights out" for one hour earlier than the first night. By then, much of the excitement of arriving and being away from home will have lessened. And after a full day of teaching and activity, your youth will be ready to sleep much earlier than on day one.

Chapter Three QUALITIES OF A GREAT RETREAT LEADER

No matter how sophisticated your program may be, the success or failure of a retreat is largely dependent on the qualities displayed by the retreat leader. Each of us have our own distinct styles of leadership, but I've found six qualities that can greatly enhance anyone's ability to lead effective retreats:

A great retreat leader is a *visionary*

If someone asked you, "How do you know if your retreat will be a success?" how would you answer? A great leader can picture the desired outcome of any given retreat and diligently work toward that outcome. Out of vision and energy, passion and commitment are born. I agree with Solomon when he says in Proverbs 29:18: "Where there is no vision, the people perish."

A great retreat leader *sees the potential*

Much like Jesus, who saw the incredible potential in the bumbling, bragging Peter, we should strive to recognize the potential in our kids and staff. Retreats often afford us the chance to allow people to shine and flourish in a sea of encouragement and emotional safety. An effective retreat leader works hard to create an atmosphere that can propel people to achieve the objectives prayerfully set before the retreat.

A great retreat leader demonstrates *flexibility*

Anyone who has spent even the slightest time in youth ministry knows that things rarely go as planned. Retreats are no exceptions. A great retreat leader prepares in advance to meet the unexpected with a sense of quiet expectation, trusting God for guidance and direction. Whether it's losing the keys to the van in the snow, forgetting the guitar, or leaving your teaching notes at home (I've done all three and more), God is sovereign and always creates wonderful gems out of these rough times.

A great retreat leader is *decisive*

One of the greatest examples of leadership in the Bible is portrayed in Joshua 24, when Joshua calls out the people to faithfully serve the Lord. His example of courage, obedience, and confidence all reveal the decisiveness of a godly leader. Running retreats often puts *the leader* in the position of total dependence—everyone is totally dependent on *them!* A great retreat leader exercises confident, decisive direction, particularly when choices have to be made. Put your confidence in the Lord, and he will direct your steps and grant you wisdom in your time of need.

A great retreat leader is *enthusiastic*

From the time the kids arrive at the church until the last ones are picked up by their parents, a retreat leader is on display. While others may be able to dodge the responsibility or the limelight, the retreat leader must be aware of what is happening at any given time. These are valuable times to model Christlike behavior to our young people, who are watching our every smile or scowl to determine how real our faith is. Without being hypocritical, a great retreat leader works hard to stay as positive as possible to model the kind of behavior he or she wants students to emulate. Whether unpacking in three feet of snow or setting up tents in 35mph wind, a great retreat leader recognizes these situations as opportunities to model Christlike behavior and attitudes.

A great retreat leader is a *servant*

Are you one of those youth pastors who likes to teach and lead worship, but that's basically the extent of your servant's heart? Your kids will pick up that attitude real quick! A great retreat leader is willing to do anything that he or she would ask someone else to do. Jesus modeled this for us in John 13 when he demonstrated the fullness of his love by washing the apostles' feet. A great retreat leader "washes" the feet of his or her staff and young people as he or she packs the vans, picks up trash, tears down tents, and carries luggage for others. Kids may forget what the speaker taught them, but they'll never forget what a servant-minded retreat leader showed them.

Retreats don't just happen. There are times when spur-of-the-moment events or unexpected changes can create memorable experiences; but for the most part, retreats require a great deal of planning and preparation. A lack of organization will usually damage the outcome of your retreat. Your adult leaders will know that things did not go well. And your kids will know it too. Here are seven Ps to remember in organizing a successful retreat:

Purpose

Before you begin plotting the details of your retreat, determine its purpose. Hold a brainstorming session and ask yourself and your staff the following questions:

> Why are we doing this retreat?
> What outcome do we want?
> What students are we trying to reach?
> Where are our kids in their spiritual development?
> Is our purpose consistent with our ministry objectives?
> Will our pastor and the parents support this retreat?

Once each of these questions has been answered, use the responses to write a purpose statement of your retreat. Then, as a group, follow Nehemiah and his friend's example as they began their good work (Nehemiah 2:18).

Pray

Ask the Lord to show you and your staff the direction your retreat should take. Ask for his guidance in choosing a speaker and for the fulfillment of your selected purpose. Once the initial preparations have been made, ask parents, the church staff, and the students to begin praying for the retreat while it is still months away. During the retreat itself, ask people who remain in your community to pray for you while you're away.

Plan

Begin your planning at least four months in advance. I find it helpful to set aside a day or two each year just to outline retreats for the following year. Use these annual planning notes as you prepare for each retreat. Here are some questions for you and your staff to consider as you begin planning:

> How many students do we have room for at this retreat?
> What are the budgeted revenues and expenses?
> How many volunteer leaders will we need?
> What do we need to do to train the volunteers?

What events will we include to make sure there is a proper balance of social, spiritual, and recreational activities?

Does the date we've chosen compete with proms or other school events?

How often should we meet to continue our planning process?

Who will be in charge of each area of responsibility?

Once you've answered these basic questions, meet regularly to ensure each person is progressing with his or her area of responsibility. Not only does careful planning produce a more meaningful retreat, it also builds stronger relationships among volunteers and staff prior to the event itself.

Promote

Honor your programs and your kids with excellence in advertising. Prepare fliers and mailings that are appealing and will draw kids to your event. Make sure kids who may have strayed away from the group are informed. In addition to printed materials, put on skits during your youth group meetings, make promotional announcements in church, and ask kids to spread the word to their friends. Chances are, you'll miss many kids if you use just one source of promotion. Attendance will increase as you increase the number of avenues you use to advertise the retreat.

Two great resources that can help you to successfully promote your retreats and other youth ministry activities are *Great Promotion and Publicity Ideas for Youth Ministry* by Les Christie and *The Youth Workers Promo Kit* by the Church Art Works, both available from Youth Specialties. (The toll-free order number is 1-800-366-7788.)

Prepare

Jesus taught that the wise builder made a careful inventory before he began building. So should we. Nothing can ruin a retreat faster than arriving at the campsite without the food, or discovering that you were really supposed to go *north* on Highway 395, not south. The *How to Prepare a Great Retreat* and the *Retreat Checklist* appendices on pages 161 and 169 have been included to help you prepare for your trip. Go through them thoroughly several months before your event, as well as periodically before you leave. This will allow you plenty of time to obtain equipment or materials you may need.

Play

Be sure to plan some fun time into your retreat schedule. Retreats are not only times for learning and growing in the Lord; they are times for building social skills and having fun with one another. In addition to scheduled games, skits, and contests, allow free time for optional activities. Make sure that there are a range of options available. (During a typical weekend retreat, Saturday afternoon is the best time for "free time" recreation and fun events.)

Photograph

Finally, don't forget the cameras. After all the time you and your staff spend planning a retreat, be sure to capture it with photographs and videos that your kids can use for reminiscing. Displaying the photos of your retreat a few weeks after the event will make the memories come alive again. Ask a volunteer or a student who is into photography and/or video to take pictures throughout the retreat. Make sure everyone is photographed at least once. While it is likely the most popular kids will be featured more often, instruct your photographer to include everyone as equally as possible. Seeing the photos afterwards might even encourage those who did not attend to consider going on the next retreat.

SECTION TWO

GREAT RETREATS
FOR
YOUTH GROUPS

I'VE GOT A NEW ATTITUDE

Jim Burns

THE BIG IDEA

Young believers and/or those interested in the Christian faith will see how God can and will change their attitudes about some of the key issues in the Christian life.

WHO SHOULD ATTEND

All new Christians, young Christians, and students interested in the Christian faith are encouraged to attend. Each attendee is encouraged to bring along a same-sex Christian peer to strengthen this time and provide support.

LOCATION

A cabin or retreat site large enough to accommodate your group.

TIME FRAME

Friday evening through Sunday afternoon

WHAT TO BRING

✓ Sleeping bag
✓ Toiletries
✓ Bible
✓ Notebook
✓ Pen or pencil

NECESSARY INGREDIENTS

★ Recipe cards (one per person)
★ Videos: *On Thin Ice* (Side by Side) and
   God Views with Curt Cloninger (Gospel Films)
★ TV monitor and VCR
★ Meals (two breakfasts, one lunch, one dinner)
★ Snacks
★ Extra Bibles
★ Keys (one for each student)
★ Videotape of sexy TV commercials
★ Sexy magazine ads
★ Sheets of paper for Teaching #2
★ Board games

SCHEDULE

FRIDAY

[**Note:** All participants to eat dinner before arriving at church]

6:00 p.m.	Arrive at church
8:00 p.m.	Arrive at site; unload and check in
9:00 p.m.	Opening session: Recipe for Life
10:00 p.m.	Snack
10:30 p.m.	Video: *On Thin Ice*
11:30 p.m.	Discussion
12:00 a.m.	In bed
12:30 a.m.	Lights out

SATURDAY

7:30 a.m.	Wake up
8:00 a.m.	Light self-serve breakfast (cereal, fruit, rolls)
9:00 a.m.	Quiet time
9:30 a.m.	Teaching #1: A New Attitude toward Myself, My Family, and My Friends
11:00 a.m.	Individual reflection
11:05 a.m.	Group sharing
11:20 a.m.	Prayer
11:30 a.m.	Break
12:30 p.m.	Lunch
1:30 p.m.	Structured break
4:00 p.m.	Free time
6:00 p.m.	Dinner
7:00 p.m.	Reflections and light sharing
7:15 p.m.	Praise and worship
7:30 p.m.	Teaching #2: A New Attitude toward Sex, Love, and Dating

SATURDAY

8:40 p.m.	Individual reflection
8:45 p.m.	Group sharing and questions
9:30 p.m.	Prayer
10:00 p.m.	Games
11:30 p.m.	In bed
12:00 a.m.	Lights out

SUNDAY

7:30 a.m.	Wake up
8:30 a.m.	Breakfast
9:15 a.m.	Quiet time
9:45 a.m.	Teaching #3: A New Attitude toward God, the Bible, and Church
10:55 a.m.	Individual reflection
11:00 a.m.	Prayer
12:00 p.m.	Pack and load
1:00 p.m.	Depart (lunch on the road)

RETREAT COMPONENTS

FRIDAY

9:00-10:00 p.m. Opening session: Recipe for Life

This is an exercise in which those attending are challenged to consider what is really important in life. Open by reading a recipe for a favorite food (chocolate chip cookies for example), including the necessary teaspoons, pinches, cups, etc. When you've finished, hand out pencils and 3-by-5 recipe cards to each student. Ask them to create their own "Recipe for Life," and include, proportionally, the ingredients they feel are important to have a great life. Allow twenty to thirty minutes for the exercise to be completed. When everyone has finished, have each person read his or her recipe to the group. (Just like any good recipe, they are allowed to modify them!)

10:00-10:30 p.m. Snack

Fruit, ice cream, drinks. They will be hungry and need a break before the video.

10:30-11:30 p.m. Video

I recommend showing a Christian video at this time. A good selection is *On Thin Ice* (Side by Side), because it accurately depicts the challenges non-Christians go through as they weigh the decision whether or not to become a Christian. The new believers on the retreat will find it refreshingly funny and a good point of reference for the rest of the weekend.

11:30 p.m.-12:00 a.m. Discussion

After you've watched the video, ask the following questions:

"What was the best part of the video?"

"Could you identify with the lead character?"

"Do you know Christians who act like the other characters in the film?"

"How does it make you feel when some Christians think that they have license to sin because they are forgiven?"

"Do you think the lead character will become a Christian?"

9:00-9:30 a.m. Quiet time

Have students read Psalm 51 and Philippians 2 and write a one paragraph summary of each chapter. When they have finished this exercise, they should answer the following questions in their notebooks:

> According to Psalm 51:12, what does David want God to give back to him?
> Why do you think he asks for this?
> What does this tell you about the consequences of disobedience?
> According to Philippians 2, how does Paul say we should view ourselves?
> Do you have a friend or relative to whom you feel superior?
> How can you serve or honor that person this week?

9:30-11:00 a.m. Teaching #1: A New Attitude toward Myself, My Family, and My Friends

Part I: A New Attitude toward Myself

Open by showing some or all of the video *God Views* (Gospel Films), in which Curt Cloninger characterizes seven commonly-held misconceptions of God. After you've shown the video, ask, "How many of you could relate to one or more of the sketches? What are other common misconceptions of God?"

After several have shared, read 2 Corinthians 5:17 and Ephesians 6:17a, emphasizing that as new creations we have a new perspective and outlook on many of the issues of life than we had previously held. This is the basis for the whole retreat: God has given us a new attitude!

Next, pass out paper and pencils to each student. Have them write the answers to the following questions:
> "How did you think of yourself before you became a Christian?"
> "How did you determine your identity (e.g., your friends, car, clothes, sports)?"

When everyone has finished, invite several students to share their answers (allow five to eight minutes). When the sharing has finished, point out the similarity in answers (most will say their identity was found in what they did).

Point out that our identity as Christians is found in:
> Jesus Christ (Colossians 3:3)
> His Death (Galatians 2:20)

His Resurrection (Romans 6:4).

The difference between Christians and non-Christians is this: As non-believers, we found our identity and self-image in what *we* did; as believers, we find our identity and self-image in what *he* did. Ask, "What are one or two things that have changed in your self-image since you have become a Christian?" Have a few volunteers share their answers aloud.

After the students have shared, read Psalm 139:14. Ask, "Since we know that God sees us as wonderful, how does that help us to develop a godly self-image?" Again, have them share their answers out loud.

Next, divide the students into small groups with at least one adult leader in each group. Direct them to answer the following question: "How does God want you to see yourself?" Have them share their answers in their small groups.

Part II: A New Attitude toward My Family
Open this segment by pointing out how the media (television, movies, MTV) portrays parent-teen relationships. Do teens in these portrayals typically obey their parents and respect them? Not! Give specifics.

Point out three lies the media tells us:
1. Parents are to be obeyed as long as it is convenient.
2. Teens have rights and privileges equal to their parents.
3. Parents just don't understand teenagers.

Next, read Exodus 20:12. Explain that to <u>honor</u> is to esteem or respect another. Ask the students, "On a scale of one to ten, with ten being the highest, how much do you honor your parent(s)? What can you do specifically next week to honor your parent(s)?" Challenge each student to be accountable to one other person for following through on these plans.

Part III: A New Attitude toward My Friends
Have the students answer "true" or "false" to the following statements as you read each one aloud:
1. I consider my friends' needs before I consider my own.
2. I am willing to listen rather than talk.
3. I have friends who I have nothing in common with.
4. I regularly reach out to help someone who may need a word of encouragement.
5. I like to have things my way when I'm with my friends.
6. I seldom have my feelings hurt by my friends.

Remind your kids that a commonly communicated philosophy among young people is a "What's in it for me" attitude toward friendships. Is this a biblical concept?

Next, read John 5:13 and Philippians 2:1-5. Ask, "How do those verses contrast with the world's views of friendship? What can you do next week to consider others as more important than yourself, and lay down your life for your friends?" Encourage each student to be accountable to another for following through on this plan.

11:00-11:05 a.m. Individual reflection

Allow five minutes at the conclusion of this time for students to write any thoughts or feelings in their notebooks about how God may have touched them or shown them something during this session.

11:05-11:20 a.m. Group sharing

Ask the students to share aloud any thoughts they have about the changes they are making in their lives. Ask them if there are any issues that they don't understand, or if there are any scenarios they are facing when they go home that they would like to talk to the group about. Encourage the students to talk to one other as they share and problem solve.

11:20-11:30 a.m. Prayer

Select one person to lead a closing prayer, preferably a peer leader. Choose the person in advance. Encourage the prayer leader to seek the Lord specifically regarding the issues that have surfaced during the sharing time.

1:30-4:00 p.m. Structured break

Plan specific activities for this time period. Include a variety of options: team sports, a shopping trip, a musicians' jam, a biking expedition, etc.

4:00-5:00 p.m. Free time

Gather everyone at your site, but do not have anything planned. Allow time for homework, rest, or just lounging around.

7:30-8:40 p.m. Teaching #2: A New Attitude toward Sex, Love, and Dating

[Note: Allow plenty of time during this session for questions regarding sexual standards, masturbation, and other issues. Be prepared to answer these questions, or teach directly on the subject. Since these matters are delicate, you will have to determine your standards. Consult your senior pastor, parent board, and other youth workers as you prepare for this section. Also, allocate time for the students to process what they are hearing, possibly for the first time. If possible, bring at least one man and one woman on this retreat who are equipped to counsel kids who may be experiencing a variety of emotions as they are confronted with their past sins and other emotional baggage they have been carrying.]

Open with a contest to see who can list the most popular songs that talk about love, sex, or dating. Next, play the video of sexy TV commercials you prepared ahead of time; then pass around magazine ads you clipped and brought with you that glorify sex and sensuality.

Now introduce the students to the Three Misconceptions About Sex:

Misconception #1: God Hates Sex
God created sex and our sexuality. He thinks it's great! But its expression is reserved for those who have committed their lives in love in the covenant of marriage (see Matthew 19:4-6).

Misconception #2: Everyone is Doing It
Research indicates that anywhere between forty to fifty percent of high school students *aren't* having sex.

Misconception #3: Christians Aren't Tempted Sexually
Jesus was tempted in all things, yet without sin. We can expect to be sexually tempted; yet we know that God provides a way out (see 1 Cor. 10:13).

Next, put pieces of paper around the room with one of the "bases" listed below on each sheet of paper:
> Looking at the other person
> Holding hands
> Holding hands constantly
> Hugging
> Caressing
> Light kissing
> French kissing
> Fondling of the breasts
> Fondling of the genitals
> Oral sex
> Sexual intercourse

Ask, one at a time, the following questions:
> "How far is too far if you're just friends?"
> "How far is too far on a first date?"
> "How far is too far if you're going steady?"

"How far is too far if you're engaged?"

After asking each question, have the students stand next to the answer that reflects the furthest that one should go in that particular relationship. Do not comment on the voting; it may deter people from honestly expressing their opinions.

Now, discuss with the students the need to set physical standards in their relationships *before* they are in the back seat of the car! A youth pastor in my community met with his then girlfriend at McDonald's to discuss their physical relationship. When they married, they were both virgins! This is also a good time to let the kids hear from you and your staff about how you have handled your previous and present relationships.

8:40-8:45 p.m. Individual reflection
Allow five minutes at the conclusion of this time for students to write any thoughts or feelings in their notebooks about how God may have touched them or shown them something during this session.

8:45-9:30 p.m. Group sharing and questions
Young people are always curious about their sexuality and will undoubtedly have questions about the issues you have raised, particularly as new Christians. Allow plenty of time for this, patiently responding to their queries. You should come prepared to discuss *your* own feelings about physical standards in dating relationships, as well as masturbation.

Following the question-and-answer time, address the issue of "secondary virginity," or beginning over again as a new Christian. A good opening might be: "Some of you are wondering tonight if it is too late for you since you have been sexually active. Some of you may have experienced an abortion, date rape, or some other traumatic experience that relates to your sexuality and sexual identity." At this time, read 2 Corinthians 5:17 and 1 John 1:9 twice. It is vital to slowly and sensitively help all present to see that our God is a God of second chances, and that they can become virgins again.

This often leads to a time of prayer and ministry, particularly with the girls. Let kids know that there will be adults available to talk with during the game time if they want to talk through some personal concerns. Prepare your staff in advance for this possibility. [**Note:** Be prepared to make some counseling referrals when you return from the retreat.]

Close this time with what I call the "Radical Respect" challenge. Open with a statement like, "Did you ever consider that every Christian has the spirit of Jesus living in them? The people you date and the person you eventually marry has the spirit of Christ in them! To radically respect someone is to treat them as better than yourself, as if you were dating Jesus!" Read Philippians 2:3-5 and ask those present to take the challenge to radically respect all of their current and future dating relationships with a commitment to sexual purity (see 1 Thes. 4:3).

9:30-10:00 p.m. Prayer

To those who take the challenge, close in an extended time of prayer, asking God to give them patience, wisdom, and self control in their dating relationships. Encourage willing students to offer their prayers of commitment aloud. Following this time of prayer, give each responding student a key that is to represent their commitment to purity. The key is to be given to their spouse on their wedding day. It represents the commitment they made to save themselves for the person they have honored with the covenant relationship of marriage. (Many locksmiths have extra keys, but you may wish to spend a little bit more to buy some nice keys and build that cost into the retreat.)

10:00-11:30 p.m. Games

Bring out some board games and other game ideas that the kids can play. Encourage all of your adult leadership staff to stay up and join in the fun, as this helps build student/leader bonds.

9:15-9:45 a.m. Quiet time

Have the students read Psalm 100; 1 Corinthians 9:24-27; and 2 Corinthians 5:17-21. Encourage them to pray about their commitments to sexual purity they made the night before. Let them know that you're available if they have any further questions about last night's teaching.

9:45-10:55 a.m. Teaching #3: A New Attitude toward God, the Bible, and Church

This session is interactive and more of a discussion than a lecture.

Part I: Developing a New Attitude toward God

Lead a discussion with the following questions:

"How did you think of God before you became a Christian?"

"How does the media (music, MTV, movies) portray the image of God?"

"Are these accurate? If so, how? If not, why not?"

"How do you see God now that you are a Christian?"

Point out that the Bible describes God in many ways. Have students read the following verses out loud, then tell them the corresponding word that describes that aspect of God:

2 Peter 3:9 (patient)

John 3:16 (loving)

Philippians 1:6 (faithful)

1 John 1:9 (forgiving)

Psalm 70:5 (our help)

Hebrews 13:8 (unchanging)

Part II: Developing a New Attitude toward the Bible

Now, begin a discussion with the following questions:

"What did you think of the Bible before you became a Christian?"

"How do you think of the Bible now?"

Point out what the Bible says about itself:

The Word is Jesus Christ (John 1:1)

It is living and active (Hebrews 4:12)

It is sharper than a two-edged sword (Hebrews 4:12)

It is God-breathed and useful (2 Timothy 3:16-17)

Part III: Developing a New Attitude toward Church
Continue your discussion with these questions:
"How did you think about church before you became a Christian?"
"Has your perspective changed? If so, how?"

Now share what the Bible says about the church:
Church is where people share and help each other (Acts 2:44)
It is to be marked by unity and care (1 Corinthians 12:25-26)
It is not to be neglected (Hebrews 10:25)
The church is people, not a place (Matthew 18:20)

Ask if there are any more questions concerning any of the material just covered. When finished, conclude with a closing prayer.

10:55-11:00 a.m. Individual reflection
Allow five minutes at the conclusion of this time for students to write any thoughts or feelings in their notebooks about how God may have touched them or shown them something during this session.

11:00-11:30 a.m. Prayer
Have the students form a large circle, joining hands. Lead an extended time of prayer, encouraging students to pray aloud concerning the commitments and goals that they have set during the weekend. Encourage them to keep their prayers short and to the point so that all of the students have an opportunity to pray. Ask them also to pray for one another's goals and commitments. Remind them that we are only successful at the Christian life when we're living it under God's power, not our own.

Conclude your prayer with a group hug.

THE ULTIMATE 39½ HOURS

Chris Cannon

THE BIG IDEA

A retreat designed to help high school or junior high guys decide between being a man of the world or a man after God's own heart.

WHO SHOULD ATTEND

All high school or *all* junior high guys. The retreat works best with at least ten guys and no more than twenty-four.

LOCATION

A local home that will accommodate the group size. A home with a pool is ideal.

TIME FRAME

Friday evening through Sunday afternoon

WHAT TO BRING

- ✓ Sleeping bag
- ✓ Toiletries
- ✓ Athletic clothes
- ✓ Swimsuit (if pool is available and it's the right season)
- ✓ Bible
- ✓ Notebook
- ✓ Pen or pencil

NECESSARY INGREDIENTS

- ★ Pizza
- ★ Soft drinks
- ★ Three meals (two breakfasts, one dinner)
- ★ Easel with chalkboard or white board
- ★ Videotaped TV commercials depicting "macho" men
- ★ Pre-selected "male image" magazine advertisements
- ★ Name tags
- ★ Sports videos
- ★ Snack foods
- ★ Gatorade
- ★ Copies of the *Covenant to Live as a Godly Man* (found on page 45)
- ★ Dessert for Saturday night
- ★ Video camera
- ★ VCR and TV monitor
- ★ Camera for group picture
- ★ Sporting equipment
- ★ Adult drivers

SCHEDULE

FRIDAY

8:00 p.m.   Meet at adult leader's house
8:30 p.m.   Activity and pizza
10:00 p.m.   Teaching #1: Images
11:00 p.m.   Overview of the weekend
11:30 p.m.   Free time
12:00 a.m.   In bed
1:00 a.m.   Lights out

SATURDAY

9:00 p.m.   Concert of prayer
9:30 p.m.   Dessert
10:00 p.m.   Award ceremony and video of the day's events
10:30 p.m.   Free time
12:00 a.m.   Crash!

SATURDAY

7:30 a.m.   Wake up
8:00 a.m.   Breakfast
9:30 a.m.   Devotional
10:00 a.m.   Miniature golf, batting cages and other recreation
12:30 p.m.   Fast food lunch
1:30 p.m.   Leave for athletic field or court
2:00 p.m.   Team sport (basketball, ultimate frisbee or touch football)
3:15 p.m.   Refreshment break (ideally Gatorade)
3:30 p.m.   Head back to the house
4:00 p.m.   Showers, relaxing, and swimming if pool is available (have sports videos on)
6:00 p.m.   Dinner
7:15 p.m.   Praise and worship
7:45 p.m.   Teaching #2: Seven Mistakes Men Make and How to Avoid Them

SUNDAY

7:30 a.m.   Wake up
8:00 a.m.   Breakfast (self-serve)
8:45 a.m.   Begin cleaning and packing
9:30 a.m.   Teaching #3: Heart Checkup
10:30 a.m.   Testimonies
11:00 a.m.   Group covenant to be godly men
11:30 a.m.   Group prayer, hugs, and picture
12:00 p.m.   Finish cleaning
12:30 p.m.   Parents arrive to pick up the kids

RETREAT COMPONENTS

FRIDAY

8:30-10:00 p.m. Activity and pizza

Put the names of famous men (the more macho the better), real or fictional, on 8½-by-11 inch pieces of paper. Then tape one name on the back of each guy. When you say, "Go," the guys mingle. Their task is to figure out whose name is taped on their back. They do this by approaching other guys, letting those guys see the names on their back, and asking up to three questions of that person about the name on their back. The person answering can respond with only yes or no. Bring enough names to do two rounds.

When you've finished the activity, pause for a short pizza and soda break.

10:00-11:00 p.m. Teaching #1: Images

Pass around magazine advertisements you've clipped out that depict men in a variety of images. Follow this up with TV commercials you've videotaped which feature men. (Put in a few silly ones to help break the initial ice!) Following each picture or commercial, ask the boys what image of men is being portrayed. Write these down on an easel or have someone else record the answers. When you've finished, review the answers that were shared.

Now divide the guys into small groups, with an adult facilitator for each group. Have each group list the names of several men (both in the Bible or otherwise) whom they consider to be godly men, along with the qualities that they feel these men possess that gives them their godly character. When everyone is done, have a student from each group read back their names and the qualities they identified in those men. Listen for common denominators throughout the sharing and record these on your easel.

When all groups have shared, ask each guy to pick two of the qualities on the board that he would like to possess. Lead in prayer for your guys that they would develop these characteristics.

11:00-11:30 p.m. Overview

Share the following goals for the weekend with your guys:
Examine how the world defines manhood and contrast that with the biblical standard for men.
Have a whole lot of fun!

Learn from the mistakes that seven Old Testament men made, and how we can avoid and overcome those mistakes in our own lives.
Examine the wellspring of life with a "heart check."

You might not want to divulge all the activities they'll participate in, because the element of surprise is valuable with a bunch of guys. I include a quick character sketch of Timothy to help set the tone of the weekend. You can bring out several important qualities of Timothy's life to encourage the guys to take their faith more seriously:

Timothy's age
Many scholars believe he was probably in his late teens at the time of Paul's letters to him
His responsibilities
Overseer of many churches (1 Timothy 1:3, 4)
His challenges
Overcoming obstacles regarding his age (1 Timothy 4:12, 13)
Overcoming his timidity (2 Timothy 1:7)
Teaching others (2 Timothy 1:1, 2)

In Titus 2:6-8, Paul makes several challenges to the young men with whom Titus has responsibility over. Read this text out loud and ask your guys to identify these challenges. Some points you will want to be sure to bring out include:

To be self-controlled (vs. 6)
To have integrity (A good definition is being the same person you are in private as you are in church, vs. 7)
To be serious (vs. 7)
To use sound speech (vs. 8)

Ask, "Why do you think Paul gave these exhortations to these young men in particular? Are they still relevant and applicable to young men today?"

11:30 p.m.-12:00 a.m. Free time and snacks
Allow for pillow fights and mild roughhousing, yet be sensitive to the guys who won't participate in this time. Adult involvement in this kind of play time is valuable to model responsible "goofing off."

1:00 a.m. Lights out
Allow for a later bed time the first night due to the high energy level!

9:30-10:00 a.m. Devotional

Read through the "Proverb of the Day." As the book of Proverbs is broken into thirty-one chapters, read the chapter that correlates to the day's date. Read it together with each boy reading a verse aloud, or have them read it together in small groups of three or four. Discuss what part of the proverb best represents the qualities of a godly man.

10:00 a.m.-12:30 p.m. Miniature golf, batting cages, and other recreation

The goal here is to have a great time with a lot of laughs. Create competitions or just have fun playing miniature golf, batting cages, air hockey, or other activities. Encourage your adult staff to help foster the right atmosphere of lightheartedness. Warn your adult staff not to get *too* competitive with the students.

12:30-1:30 p.m. Fast food lunch

Before you begin your morning recreation time, take lunch orders. About one hour prior to your arrival, phone in your order to a nearby fast food restaurant. This will allow for more playing time and less waiting time—and the restaurant will thank you!

2:00-3:15 p.m. Team sport

Select a team game that will work for the size and makeup of your group, such as touch football, ultimate frisbee, or basketball. Elect team captains who will be encouragers to all the guys on their teams. Choose the teams fairly and set some ground rules about sportsmanship. Most of all, have a good time and encourage one another as you play.

3:15-3:30 p.m. Refreshment break

Be sure to have lots of Gatorade. Use this time to encourage the guys who weren't superstars or didn't score the points. Notice the things that they did right and encourage them in those things.

4:00-5:30 p.m. Showers, relaxing, and swimming (if pool is available)

Run sports videos while the kids are lounging around. Adults should shower last, no matter how badly they need it.

6:00-6:45 p.m. Dinner
Barbecuing is ideal. It's easy and guys are very forgiving!

7:15-7:45 p.m. Praise and Worship
Begin with fast songs like "King Jesus is All," "I've Got a River of Life," and "How Majestic is Your Name." Next, move into slower worship songs like "Bless the Lord," "Glorify Thy Name," "You Are My Hiding Place," and "I Love You Lord."

7:45-9:00 p.m. Teaching #2: Seven Mistakes Men Make and How to Avoid Them
This is a fun and challenging look at the mistakes that seven men of the Old Testament made, with a verse from Proverbs that corresponds to each particular shortcoming.

Mistake #1: Knowing the right thing to do and not doing it
This was the mistake of Adam (see Proverbs 29:18). He was there in the garden when Eve was being tempted, and he had already received instruction from God, yet Adam did nothing to prevent the Fall. Use a recent event to illustrate this, a sin of omission where a wrong was committed and no one intervened.

Mistake #2: Making decisions based on appearances
This was the mistake of Lot (see Proverbs 3:5-7). When Abram and Lot came to a crossroads in Genesis 13:8-13, Abram let Lot decide where he would go to live. Lot chose what looked good, but it turned out to be Sodom. I use an illustration about buying a used 1961 Chrysler because it looked so cool, but only ran for three weeks. I made a decision based on appearance. Other Scriptures you can use here include 1 Samuel 16:7 and Luke 16:15.

Mistake #3: Making excuses to evade responsibilities
This was the mistake of Moses (see Proverbs 16:25). Exodus 3-4 recounts the five reasons Moses gave God as to why he couldn't be God's chosen leader:
>   1. He's nobody (3:11)
>   2. The Israelites won't believe that God sent him (3:13)
>   3. The Israelites won't believe that the Lord appeared to him (4:1)
>   4. He's not a good speaker (4:10)
>   5. He just doesn't want to do it (4:13)

[**Note:** This is a time for your guys to hear of your confidence in them. Read 1 Timothy 4:12 and Numbers 11:23 as verses to strengthen them.]

Mistake #4: Raising willful, disobedient children

This was the mistake of Samuel (see Proverbs 22:6 and 17:6). Read 1 Samuel 8:1-5, which recounts why Saul would eventually be chosen king of Israel. Ask, "If Samuel was such a godly man, why didn't his sons take his place?" This is a powerful time as several guys are bound to express common themes in our culture: "Dad doesn't have time for me" or "My father doesn't live at home." Ask something like, "What advice would you give to a new father about raising his son?" You will be impressed with their thoughtful and sincere answers.

Mistake #5: Fearing the rejection of men rather than seeking the approval of God

This was the mistake of Saul (see Proverbs 29:25). Saul was the ultimate people pleaser, which ultimately lead to his removal as king. Read 1 Samuel 15, emphasizing verses 24 and 30 as examples of his fear of rejection and humiliation in front of the people of Israel. Follow this Scripture by leading a brief discussion on the importance of peer acceptance in your guys' lives.

Mistake #6: The inability to delay gratification

This was the mistake of David (see Proverbs 6:25-29). Read the account of David and Bathsheba in 2 Samuel 11. Ask, "What are the temptations that guys deal with that are hard to control? What can happen when we give in to temptation? What happened to David?"

Next, read the account of Esau giving up his birthright for a cup of stew in Genesis 25:29-35. Ask, "Why did Esau 'despise his birthright' (vs. 34)? What can we sacrifice to satisfy our immediate desires?" Close by reading Ephesians 5:22-23, outlining the fruits of the Spirit.

Mistake #7: The willingness to tolerate evil

This was the mistake of Jehosophat (see Proverbs 8:13; 15:9; 25:26). Read 2 Chronicles 20:32-33, pointing out how King Jehosophat did what was right in God's eyes *except* that the high places (idols) were not removed. Ask, "What are the 'high places' (idols) in the lives of high school guys? In our lives? Why is it hard to give these up to the Lord?"

9:00-9:30 p.m. Concert of Prayer

When finished with the teaching, allow for a minute or two of silent reflection. Then lead in a time of directed prayer. Request that the prayers be short to allow everyone to participate. Direct your guys to pray specifically for God's help in the "mistake areas" of their own lives.

9:30-10:30 a.m. Teaching #3: Heart Checkup

Open with questions like:

"How important is your heart?"

"Could you live without it?"

"What leads to heart problems?"

"How vital is it to maintain a good diet to have a healthy heart?"

Read Proverbs 4:23. Ask questions like, "What leads to spiritual cholesterol? What kind of spiritual 'diet' do we need to maintain a healthy heart for Christ?"

Read 1 John 2:16-17. Identify areas of temptation listed in this passage that can lead to a spiritual "hardening of the arteries" (craving, lust, pride, greed).

Conclude this session with a reflective song of worship (such as "Refiner's Fire") and a time of brief prayer that allows the guys to seek forgiveness for where they have fallen prey to the desires of the world.

10:30-11:00 a.m. Testimonies

Briefly review the weekend's teachings. Then open up the floor for a time of sharing and testimonies. Allow guys to share briefly on what God has shown them about living a godly life.

11:00-11:30 a.m. Group covenant to be godly men

Display and read the covenant found on page 45. Have a copy of the covenant on hand for each guy to sign as an indication of his commitment to be a man of God. Each covenant has signature spaces reserved for two witnesses. These witnesses become accountability partners for the signer. Encourage them to carefully choose who they will ask to be their witnesses; the three (the signer and his two witnesses) are to meet every other week for six months after the retreat to discuss how they are doing with their commitments to be godly men.

COVENANT
TO LIVE AS A
GODLY MAN

I, _____,

do hereby commit myself to the personal development of Christlike

character and godly integrity by keeping my heart and mind pure. I

covenant to guard my heart and my mind through regular prayer,

fellowship, worship, and the study of God's Word. It is my intention to

become a man after God's own heart.

Signed _____

Date _____

Witness _____

Date _____

Witness _____

Date _____

KNEE TO KNEE IN RENEWAL

Skip Seibel

THE BIG IDEA

1. Strengthen friendship among youth group members through group bonding, sharing, and affirming activities.
2. Ignite and fortify the youth group members' faith in Christ through talks, knee-to-knee discussion groups, and experiential worship.

WHO SHOULD ATTEND

Anyone who is interested in renewing their spiritual fervor. This retreat works best with small groups (six to twenty-four students).

LOCATION

A retreat center or a cabin in the mountains is ideal.

TIME FRAME

To achieve optimum benefit, a two-night retreat is preferable. However, the goals of this retreat can be accomplished in a one-night, one-day setting.

WHAT TO BRING

✓ Sleeping bag
✓ Toiletries
✓ Bible
✓ Notebook
✓ Pen or pencil

NECESSARY INGREDIENTS

★ Food for five meals (one dinner, two lunches, two breakfasts)
★ Snack food for break times & Saturday evening dessert (soft drinks, popcorn, chips, cookies, fruit, etc.)
★ Five nonbreakable items per small group such as socks, Nerf balls, bean bags, or pillows (small groups will run three to eight students each)
★ One box of wooden stove matches
★ Markers and two sheets of poster board per small group

(continued)

★ Glue, old magazines, scissors, and one cardboard box per person
★ One TensionGetter™ scenario, one video camera, and one videocassette for each small group
★ VCR and TV monitor
★ Paper, pencils, 3-by-5 cards, and envelopes for each student
★ One candle and holder
★ One hand-held size cross for each student (made from popsicle sticks or other simple materials)

SCHEDULE

FRIDAY

[**Note:** All participants to eat dinner before arriving at church]

6:30 p.m.	Depart from church
8:00 p.m.	Arrive at retreat site, check in, assign rooms, and explore
8:30 p.m.	Introduction
9:00 p.m.	Bonding activities
10:00 p.m.	Sharing time
10:30 p.m.	Crazy scavenger hunt
11:15 p.m.	Snack
11:45 p.m.	Club Time I
1:00 a.m.	Get ready for bed
1:30 a.m.	Lights out

SATURDAY

8:00 a.m.	Quiet time
8:30 a.m.	Breakfast
9:15 a.m.	Sharing time
10:00 a.m.	Club Time II
11:15 a.m.	Sharing time
12:30 p.m.	Servant lunch

SATURDAY

1:30 p.m.	Group activity
2:30 p.m.	Free time
5:00 p.m.	Affirmation time
6:00 p.m.	Dinner
7:00 p.m.	Club Time III
8:00 p.m.	Group videos
9:15 p.m.	Snack
9:30 p.m.	Worship
10:30 p.m.	Group affirmation
12:30 p.m.	Lights out

SUNDAY

9:00 a.m.	Quiet time
9:30 a.m.	Breakfast
10:00 a.m.	Clean and pack
10:30 a.m.	Closing worship
11:30 a.m.	Depart for home (lunch on the road)

RETREAT COMPONENTS

8:30-9:00 p.m. Introduction

Gather the students into a meeting room. Review the facility rules and recreational opportunities, then introduce your retreat goals:

1. To develop greater community and strengthen existing relationships in the youth group
2. To learn how to better minister and serve one another
3. To renew our passion, love, and service for Jesus

9:00-10:00 p.m. Bonding activities

Divide your kids into small groups with at least one adult leader per group. Then have your groups do the following activities, allowing ten to fifteen minutes for each activity.

Knots: Have each group form a circle. Each person then grabs the right hand of another person in the circle (not the person next to him or her) with his or her right hand. People then repeat the process with their left hands. The task for the group is to untangle themselves without letting go of hands. To increase the difficulty, eliminate talking.

Group Juggle: Have each group form a circle. Give an adult leader in each group five nonbreakable objects. The adult leader throws one object to someone in the circle (not next to him or her). That person throws the object to someone else (not next to him or her). This process continues until all members have caught and thrown the object one time. This is now your "juggle." The adult begins again with one object. When the group throws and catches the object without dropping it, it has successfully juggled one object. The adult leader begins again, this time throwing two objects in succession. The group continues this process until all five objects have been juggled in succession without dropping any, or until time is called.

Debrief these two bonding activities with a quick discussion, using these four questions:

"Who were the key people in solving the hand knots?"
"What did you have to do to juggle successfully?"
"What was the purpose of these two activities?"
"What do these activities teach us about groups?"

10:00-10:30 p.m. Sharing time

Bring the whole group back together for a fun, low-risk sharing time. Give one person a box of wooden stove matches. Have this person light a match and tell as much about himself or herself as he or she can before the match burns his or her finger. Continue this process until all have shared. Provide a safe disposal container for the burnt matches.

10:30-11:15 p.m. Crazy scavenger hunt ✓

Break into your small groups. Give each group this list of meaningless names:
1. Free Willy Thin Fin Flicker
2. Willy Wonka Zinger-Finger
3. Long Fuzzy Wrapper
4. Blue Dotted Hook and Hanger
5. Round Nose Zipper Zapper
6. Whatchamacallit
7. Dino Dingalong
8. Big Red Do Hicky
9. A Small Fuzz-Waz
10. A Knee Slapper

Give them fifteen minutes to find objects that they think fit the names. When the groups have returned, have each group share their items with the whole gathering. This is a fun and active group-building scavenger hunt.

11:45 p.m.-12:45 a.m. Club Time I

This main teaching time consists of group singing, a message, knee-to-knee discussion groups, and a group project. For group singing, use a song leader with a guitar or keyboard; if a musician is unavailable, sing along to worship tapes by artists like Al Denson and Petra. Then share the following message:

Significant People

Opening: Share about a person—a coach, friend, or teacher—who has had a significant, though not necessarily spiritual, impact on your life. Share one encounter with that person that greatly influenced you. Focus on one event. Be specific. Use humor if you can.

Body: Select a biblical text which depicts one person being influenced by another person, such as Zaccheus and Jesus in Luke 19:1-6, Andrew's introducing Peter to Jesus in John 1:40-42, or Barnabas bringing Paul from Tarsus to Antioch in Acts 11:25-26. Tell the story in your own words, illustrating where possible with stories and personal examples.

Conclusion: Now share with the group about a person who has had significant impact in your *faith development.* Zero in on one particular incident. Conclude by saying, "God places particular people in our lives to influence us. I now want you to share, in your small groups, the stories of people who have significantly influenced your lives."

When you have finished, have the students return to their small groups, this time knee to knee. The adult leader in each group leads the group discussion.

When the discussions are finished, give each small group a poster board and a set of marker pens. Have each small group make a poster depicting the significant people in their lives. When all the groups have finished, each group may share their poster with the whole gathering.

SATURDAY

8:00-8:30 a.m. Quiet time

Encourage the students to read a psalm, the "Proverb of the Day" (the chapter in the book of Proverbs that corresponds to the particular day of the month), and the fifth chapter of Matthew. Solitude and silence are to be maintained during the quiet time.

9:15-10:00 a.m. Sharing time

Give each student ten to fifteen minutes to find an object that represents their current relationship with Jesus. When everyone has returned, have each person share his or her item and what it represents with the whole group. This activity will help the students to focus on their relationships with God.

10:00-11:15 a.m. Club Time II

Begin with a time of singing and worship. Then share the following message:

Significant Events

Opening: Share with the students a significant event from your life—making a sports team, being caught in a wrongdoing, moving to a new community—anything that made a significant, though not necessarily spiritual, impact in your character development. Focus on one event. Be specific. Use humor if you can.

Body: Select a scriptural story that depicts a watershed event in the life of a biblical character, like Peter and the great catch in John 21, the apostles and the calming of the sea in Luke 8, or the woman at the well in John 8. Tell the story in your own words, illustrating with stories or personal examples.

Conclusion: Share with the group an event in your life that had a major impact in your *faith relationship* with Christ—a summer camp, weekend retreat, mission trip, or an answered prayer. Again be specific. Zero in on one particular event. Conclude by saying, "The many events of our lives help to mold who we are. I now want you to share in your small groups events that have influenced your lives."

Break into your knee-to-knee small groups. Have each small group member share at least one significant event in his or her life. When the discussions are finished, give each small group pens, markers, glue, and magazines. Have each group make a poster depicting the key events of their lives—a collage that includes pictures that represent individual events. When all the groups are finished, have each group share their poster and its significance with the whole gathering.

11:15 a.m.-12:30 p.m. Sharing time

Give each person a cardboard box, some glue, and a supply of old magazines. Give everyone fifteen to twenty minutes to "decorate" their boxes. On the outside, they are to glue words and pictures that represent "the me everyone sees." On the inside, they glue words and pictures that reveal "the real me." When everyone has finished, get people back into their small groups. Have each person share his or her box with the small group.

12:30-1:30 p.m. Servant lunch ✓

During this lunch, everyone may *feed* themselves, but they cannot *serve* themselves. Everyone must pour one another's milk, get one another's food, butter one another's bread, etc.

1:30-2:30 p.m. Group activity

This activity involves teamwork and coordination. Begin by finding a wall, perhaps five or six feet high. Form teams with approximately seven or eight kids on each team, and an even mix of guys and girls. Give them these instructions:

"Your job, as a team, is to help each other climb this wall as fast as you can. The team that gets all its members safely on the other side the fastest is the winner. By the way, each of you will have a physical 'challenge' that will make things a little more difficult, and force you to depend on each other to accomplish your task."

Some of the challenges that you should be sure to include :
> Blindness (blindfold one team member)
> Deafness (team members may only use hand gestures when
> communicating with this person)
> Mute (give this person a pad of paper and a pencil)
> Right leg amputee
> Paraplegic (can use only their arms)
> Left arm amputee
> One completely healthy person

You may want to tie a bandanna around a person's leg, eyes, mouth, or whatever to make the "handicap" visible, just as a real physical challenge is visible to all. Each team is timed, and the clock is not stopped until the last person scales the wall. The fastest team is the winner. This is a great activity to videotape, and will help promote your next year's retreat.

[**Note:** The wall should be no higher than six feet. Have at least one adult on both sides of the wall to insure the greatest amount of safety. You will be surprised, however, with the care they take of each other.]

Some good follow-up questions can include:
> "What did you learn in our game today?"
> "Do you have a greater appreciation for what others go through who are
> physically challenged? If so, how?"
> "What can we learn about the body of Christ (the church) through our
> game?"

2:30-5:00 p.m. Free time
If your facility does not have many free time options, you may want to shorten the free time period or plan more structured events. If appropriate, also have snack food available during free time.

5:00-6:00 p.m. Affirmation time: Character Strengths
Divide your group into pairs or threes. Give pencils and 3-by-5 cards to each pair or threesome, then have them work together to make a character strength card for each person in the entire group. They're to list at least three character strengths for each person in the group on that person's 3-by-5 card. Allow fifteen to twenty minutes for this process. When everyone has finished, gather the whole group together. Have each pair or threesome share their cards with the whole gathering.

7:00-8:00 p.m. Club Time III
Open with group singing. Then share the following message:

Journey of Faith

Opening: Share a story about a time when you betrayed a friend or were betrayed by a friend. Be specific. Draw a clear picture for the students. Convey the emotions and the sorrow you felt at the time. Use humor if you can.

Body: Tell the students that while we don't want to, we often betray our friends. Sometimes we even betray our friend Jesus by our actions. Retell Peter's betrayal and denial of Jesus in Mark 14:66-72. Use your own words. Bring the story alive with illustrations or personal experiences.

Conclusion: Share your personal journey of faith. Share with them your successes, struggles, and failures. Be specific. Conclude by saying, "Each of our relationships with Christ have high points and low points. In your small groups, I want you now to share your own faith journeys."

Divide into your knee-to-knee groups. In those groups, allow each person to share his or her personal journey of faith.

When the sharing is finished, give each group member a pencil and paper. Have each person write a prayer to God, asking him to remove an obstacle or hurdle that is hampering his or her spiritual growth. Have your students save their prayers in their Bibles as a reminder that God wants to help them overcome their particular obstacles or hurdles.

8:00-9:15 p.m. Group videos

Give each small group one of the TensionGetters™ case studies found on pages 57–60. Each group must develop, rehearse, and film a five-minute video using the TensionGetter™ as the starting point. Give each group about forty-five minutes to complete the task. When all the groups have finished, bring the entire group together to watch the the videos. After each video, have everyone debrief and discuss how that group handled their particular problem.

9:30-10:30 p.m. Worship: Peter's Reinstatement

This reflective Bible study can help your students to experience a more personal relationship with Jesus Christ. With their imaginations, and John 21:1-17 as their guide, your students can experience the call of Peter. They too can encounter the mercy and love of Jesus in a new and real way.

Create the atmosphere: Use music (songs like "Humble Thyself" and "Alleluia") and candlelight to create a quiet, reflective atmosphere. Encourage the students to use this time to be quiet and still before God.

? **Read John 21:1-17** three times in the following ways:
First reading: Have one of the leaders or students read the narrative while others read along. Using their sight, they read the encounter with Jesus.
Second reading: Have one of the leaders read the narrative again. This time, the students close their eyes and listen to the story. Using their hearing, they hear the story.
Third reading: Have one of the leaders read the narrative very slowly, pausing several times. As the leader reads, the students, with their eyes closed, attempt to recreate the scene in their minds. They strive to visualize the scene before them, the characters, the interaction, the feelings and emotions.

? **Silent reflection:** Give the students fifteen to twenty minutes to recreate the scene in their imaginations. Tell the students they need to be alone and quiet. Encourage them to go off into a room by themselves or to walk outside. Tell them, "Using your imaginations, I want you to 'become' Peter and to experience the scene as he experienced it." To help guide their time, give them the following questions:

> "What emotions did Peter experience?"
> "When have you experienced and felt similar emotions?"
> "How did Peter react?"
> "When have you reacted in a similar way?"

Share discoveries: After twenty minutes, gather the students back together. Have them share the insights they gained with each other. Share with them your insights.

? **Concrete conclusion:** Gather the students into a circle. Take one of the hand-sized crosses you have brought and approach one student, saying, "(Name), do you love me more than these?" The student then replies, "Yes, Lord, you know I do." You then respond, "Feed my sheep." Hand that student a cross to keep, pick up another cross and continue this process until all the students have participated.

Group hug: The whole group forms a circle. Each person in turn goes around the circle giving everyone a hug. Conclude with a time of prayer.

10:30 p.m.-12:30 a.m. Group affirmation

At this point in the weekend, the group is now ready for some deeper sharing. In a darkened room, with the whole group sitting on the floor, place a lit candle in front of one student. The other students affirm the person who has the candle by saying what they like about that person, a character strength they have observed, or a quality they admire. The candle moves around the circle until each person, including leaders, are affirmed. This can be a very emotional time of deep sharing.

9:00-9:30 a.m. Quiet time

Again, encourage the students to read a psalm, the "Proverb of the Day", and the sixth chapter of Matthew. Remind them to maintain solitude and silence during this time.

10:30-11:30 a.m. Closing worship

This is a time of group singing, Scripture reading, and sharing. Give students an opportunity to say what the weekend has meant to them, what they have learned about God and others this weekend, or what they intend to do to deepen their walk with God as a result of the weekend.

When the sharing is finished, form a circle and conclude with a servant prayer time. During this prayer time, no one can pray for themselves. They must pray for someone else in the group by name. Give each student an opportunity to thank God and to pray for one another.

WHO CAN YOU TURN TO?

Julie felt so alone. She was facing a tough problem and needed advice from an adult. There was no one close to her who would listen, no one to help her with her burden. Her stomach ached. She wanted to talk to her mother, but her mother had enough to worry about with the divorce and the new job. It seemed so hard to face the problem by herself. She wished she could find someone who would care enough to listen.

• How do you feel about this situation?
• What is the main issue in this situation?
• What should be done about this situation?

*Scripture Guide:		
	Genesis 43:30	Romans 12:15
	Job 2:11	Galatians 6:2
	Matthew 26:36-45	Revelation 21:4

A SCHOOL NIGHT'S SECRET MEETING

Bonnie's mother will not let her use the car for social events on school nights. If she needs to go to the library or to a meeting for church or school, the use of the car is no problem. For purely social functions, however, Bonnie's mom has made it clear that the car is off limits.

Tonight Jeff will be at a birthday party for Katrina. Bonnie has been waiting for the opportunity to meet him, and at last she will have the chance . . . except she has no way to get to Katrina's house because it is a school night. Katrina tells Bonnie that she could easily get the car by telling her mom she needs to go to the library. Bonnie agrees.

On the way to Katrina's house, Bonnie stops at the library to check out a book. She doesn't feel she is lying now, since she did go to the library.

• Was Bonnie's mother unreasonable?
• If your parents make unreasonable demands, is it okay to disobey them?
• Was Bonnie really lying?
• Did Katrina do anything wrong?
• If Bonnie would have asked you what she should do, how would you have replied?

*Scripture Guide:		
	Leviticus 19:3	Proverbs 1:8-18
	1 Samuel 3:12-13	2 Corinthians 12:14
	Psalm 1:1-2	Ephesians 6:1-4
	Psalm 37:4-5	

THE END OF A FUTURE

The "animals." That's what everyone at school called them. Barry, Brad, Aaron, Jim, and Ken were all seniors. Their contribution to this football team was vital if the team was to win the league championship—which everyone expected, even though the season was just beginning.

Despite the fact that Barry's parents were alcoholics, he was a 3.8 student and was already being recruited by a number of big-time colleges. His parents were unemployed, but Barry was looking forward to a full-ride scholarship.

Though Brad was considered one of the "animals," he was a lot different than the rest of them. He didn't drink or party. Brad was a committed Christian and had the respect of all the other guys.

The Tuesday night before the season opener, the "animals" decided to have a secret drinking party to celebrate the beginning of a great season. All of them except Brad, that is. The guys knew Brad wouldn't drink—but they needed him for an alibi. Their parents trusted Brad, and if the said they were going to Brad's, no questions would be asked. Brad didn't like the idea, but he said he'd go along with it as long as the guys agreed to let him drive. They said no. They had too much respect for Brad to want him around while they got drunk. Brad agreed to cover for them, but he didn't like it.

On the way home from the party Tuesday night, Barry's car was pulled over by the police. All of the guys were hauled down to the police station, and their parents were called. The football coach heard about it the next day and angrily dropped all the "animals" from the team. Barry's future was ruined. The schools that were recruiting him suddenly lost interest. He became so depressed he began drinking every weekend. His grades fell, and eventually he dropped out of school and became an alcoholic, just like his parents.

Brad went on to college, but he was never the same. He blamed himself for Barry's disastrous one-night drinking binge. He dropped out of church and became a real loner.

• Who is most responsible for Barry's alcoholism?
• Rank the following characters from most responsible to least responsible: Barry, Brad, Barry's parents, the football coach.
• Provide a reason for each of the rankings.

*Scripture Guide: Psalms 37:25   Matthew 18:6
                      Proverbs 20:1   Romans 2:9
                      Matthew 5:13   Galatians 5:21

THE LONER

Don wasn't stupid. He knew what everyone thought of him. The mirror doesn't lie—Don wasn't very good looking. Ha! That was a laugh; he was just plain weird looking. Everyone made fun of him. He wished he could say, "Well, I may be weird looking, but at least I get straight A's" or "Go ahead, don't be friends with me. I'll drive my Porsche by myself." But Don's folks didn't have much money and his grades were average. Don was just your basic no-one-wants-to-be-around-you type of guy. He was lonely. All Don wanted was a friend. That wasn't too much to ask for, was it? Don was very lonely—and since you're in his geometry class, and since you're the only one in class who even acts like he exists, he comes to you for advice.

- What are Don's options?
- What would you advise him to do? Why?

*Scripture Guide:

Matthew 5:46	John 13:34
Matthew 19:19	Philippians 2:3-4
Matthew 22:39	James 1:9

NEGATIVE OUTLOOK

Every time I do something wrong, my parents remind me of all the things I've done wrong in the last two years. They never forget and they seldom forgive. They always focus on the negative. I can do everything I am supposed to for three weeks in a row and they never say a word, but make one mistake and I never stop hearing about it. I don't think they've ever said a positive thing to me. It doesn't matter what I do—they're never satisfied.

Arlin, 14, Freshman

How do you feel about Arlin's statement?

Strongly Agree	Agree	Neutral	Disagree	Strongly Disagree

- If you agree, what would you add to the statement above?
- If you disagree, why?

*Scripture Guide:

Ephesians 6:4	Hebrews 8:12
Colossians 3:21	

JUST WAITING

Yes, I like the fact that my folks have money. I like having a car, a nice house, and nice clothes. I enjoy all of those things. But if my parents think I'm going to be like them, they're wrong. I've made up my mind that, when I get older, I'm not going to do the big American Dream thing. I'm not going to get a job so I can buy a house in suburbia, get my Volvo station wagon, and have 2.3 kids. As soon as I get out of college, I'm going to some third-world country, live in a tent, and give my life to helping people. I enjoy the good things in life, but I also hate what they do to me and my parents. I'm not going to let that happen. My folks would die if they knew how I really felt, so I don't tell them. I'm just waiting until I'm old enough to do what I want.

Ken, 16, Sophomore

How do you feel about Ken's statement?

Strongly Agree	Agree	Neutral	Disagree	Strongly Disagree

• If you agree, what would you add to the statement above?
• If you disagree, why?

*Scripture Guide: Matthew 19:16-24   Ephesians 6:1-3
                         Luke 6:24   Revelation 3:17

No Excuses

Chris Cannon

THE BIG IDEA

This retreat is designed to help kids recognize and overcome their fears of leadership, develop a godly standard for their lives, and formulate a strategy to utilize their skills throughout the school year. This retreat serves as an orientation for the new members of your high school student leadership team. Through this retreat you can achieve:

- Team building
- Introduction to leadership
- Training in biblical leadership skills
- Development of an action plan for the school year

WHO SHOULD ATTEND

Those high school and/or junior high school students who have been previously approved through an application process (see page 70).

LOCATION

Cabin or campground that can accommodate ten to eighteen people.

TIME FRAME

Friday night through Sunday afternoon

WHAT TO BRING

✓ Sleeping bag
✓ Toiletries
✓ Bible
✓ Notebook
✓ Pen or pencil
✓ Hiking shoes

NECESSARY INGREDIENTS

★ Food for five meals (one dinner, two lunches, two breakfasts)
★ Snack food for break times and Saturday evening dessert (soft drinks, popcorn, chips, cookies, fruit, etc.)
★ Paper and pens
★ Whiteboard and easel
★ Name tags
★ Name tags (or paper and tape) for the *Name Game*

SCHEDULE

FRIDAY

[**Note:** All participants to eat dinner before arriving at church]

6:00 p.m.	Leave church
9:00 p.m.	Arrive at cabin, unload, snack break
10:00 p.m.	The Name Game
10:15 p.m.	The Game of Questions
12:00 a.m.	Lights out

SUNDAY

7:30 a.m.	Wake up
8:00 a.m.	Breakfast
9:00 a.m.	Quiet time
10:00 a.m.	Testimonies, sharing, and group prayer
11:00 a.m.	Group hug and team picture
11:30 a.m.	Pack
12:30 p.m.	Light lunch
1:30 p.m.	Leave
4:00 p.m.	Return to church

SATURDAY

7:30 a.m.	Wake up
8:15 a.m.	Breakfast
9:00 a.m.	Quiet time
10:00 a.m.	Teaching #1: The Call of Successful Leadership
11:00 a.m.	Reflection questions and prayer
11:30 a.m.	Break
12:30 p.m.	Lunch
1:30 p.m.	Break
5:00 p.m.	Brainstorming
6:00 p.m.	Dinner
7:00 p.m.	Teaching #2: Qualities of a Great Leader
8:00 p.m.	Concert of prayer
9:30 p.m.	Faith Walk: The Steps of Faith
10:00 p.m.	Dessert
11:00 p.m.	Lights out

RETREAT COMPONENTS

FRIDAY

10:00-10:15 p.m. The Name Game

Put the names of leaders from the Bible (e.g., Moses, David, Deborah, Solomon, Nehemiah, Peter, Paul, Timothy, Priscilla, etc.) on slips of paper or adhesive name tags and attach one to the back of each student. When you say "Go," each student then asks another student three yes-or-no questions, trying to discover the name of the person on his or her own back. After they've asked three questions, they must move on to another student. The game continues until everyone has discovered their identity. If you have a large group, do this icebreaker twice to ensure that everyone is able to interact.

10:15-11:30 p.m. The Game of Questions

Each student and adult leader is given two small pieces of paper and asked to write a thought-provoking question on each of them, such as:

> When was the last time you cried, and why?
>
> Which student in this room do you admire the most?
>
> If you could be anyone in the Bible except Jesus, who would you be and why?

All the questions are put into a hat; the students draw and answer them at random. After each question is answered, the person answering passes the hat to the person of his or her choice. Complete at least two rounds. Encourage students and adults to be as honest as they can, but remember that not all of them will be on the same level of intimacy. Every answer is a good one. This has proven to be one of the consistent highlights of our retreats, frequently resulting in tears and team bonding.

9:00-10:00 a.m. Quiet time: Nehemiah 1-2

Encourage the kids to spend some time in prayer by themselves with God. As they read the Nehemiah passages, direct them to look specifically for leadership qualities that are stated in these chapters.

10:00-11:00 a.m. Teaching #1: The Call of Successful Leadership (Exodus 3-4, Joshua 1)

This teaching is designed to address the inadequacies student leaders often feel as they enter into peer ministry. While Moses was reluctant to lead, the Lord reminded him of who was really in charge.

Open this time with questions like, "How many of you are a little nervous about being in student ministry? What are some of your concerns or fears?" Take time to hear from everyone; it is usually the perfect segue into the teaching.

When everyone who wants to share has done so, say something like, "Well, Moses, who is considered one of the most respected men in the Bible, had his concerns about leadership as well. Let's take a look. Please open your Bibles to Exodus, chapter three." Read the text straight through, going around the circle with everyone reading one verse each (this keeps the group focused and involved).

Then say, "Let's take a closer look at the five excuses Moses gave God as to why he couldn't, or wouldn't, be the leader of Israel's exodus from Egypt."

Excuse #1: "Who am I?" (3:11—unworthiness)
> Ask, "Why do you think he felt this way? Have you ever felt like Moses? What were the circumstances?"
> Note God's response: "I will be with you" (vs. 12).
> Then ask, "How does God's response deal with Moses' feelings of unworthiness?"

Excuse #2: "By whose authority do I lead?" (3:13—unbelief)
> Ask, "What leads people to lack faith?"
> Note God's response: "I am who I am" (vss. 19-22).
> Then ask, "How does this answer from God relate to Moses' doubt?"

Excuse #3: "What if they don't believe me?" (4:1—fear of rejection)
> Ask, "Are you concerned that your peers won't accept you as a student leader? If so, why?"
> Note God's response: "I am able to do all things" (vss. 2-9).

Then ask, "Does this strengthen or encourage you? How?"

Excuse #4: "I can't do it!" (4:10-faithlessness)

> Ask, "Do you ever wonder if you will actually be used by God to make a difference in someone's life?"
> Note God's response: "I will help you, GO!" (vs. 12).
> Then ask, "How does God's response strengthen you?"

Excuse #5: "Send someone else!" (4:13-unwillingness)

> Ask, "What are you afraid to do? What would you rather have someone else do than yourself in student leadership?"
> Note God's response: "I will help you and give you help" (vss. 14-17).
> Then say, "God wants to use you! He could have called someone else, but, he called you!"

Now, have your group read Joshua 1:1-9, Joshua's call from God to leadership. Then say, "What four things does the Lord command Joshua to do?"

> 1. Be strong (vs. 6)
> 2. Be courageous (vs. 6)
> 3. Obey the Word (vs. 7)
> 4. Meditate on the Word (vs. 8)

Then ask, "According to verse 9, what will be the outcome be if Joshua does all four things?"

11:00-11:30 a.m. Reflection questions and prayer

When you've finished Teaching #1, break your kids into small groups with at least one adult in each small group. Have each adult volunteer lead his or her group in discussing the following questions:

> What areas do you think God wants to use you in leadership this year (e.g., teaching, prayer, evangelism, missions, newsletter, etc.)?
> Which of the five excuses that Moses used can you identify with?
> How can Joshua 1:1-9 help you to overcome any doubts or fears you may have? Be specific. (Have the students in each group pray for one another regarding their specific doubts and fears.)

12:30-1:30 p.m. Lunch

Put out all of the ingredients and packages to make sandwiches, soup, and chips, but leave them unopened and wrapped. Just as you are getting ready to prepare lunch, announce that you are taking the adult staff out to lunch (except for one adult supervisor who will remain with the kids), and that the students will need to prepare and clean up lunch on their own. Then, load up your car and leave. When you get back, find out how things went and who became the unofficial group leader. [**Note:** Leave the phone number of the restaurant you are going to be at, and take the phone number of the cabin with you.] This is an optional activity, but, if you can do it, it's worth it!

1:30-4:30 p.m. Break

Create different options for the students during this break time. Use the surroundings to help them relax and enjoy God's creation. Activities can include hiking, basketball, shopping in town, reading, napping, doing homework.

5:00-6:00 p.m. Brainstorming: church service, community service, outreach

Successful student leadership includes ownership of and involvement in the planning of your youth ministry programs by the students. This time of brainstorming is designed to do both—by giving your students a chance to express their ideas on church service projects, community service projects and regular evangelistic outreach. You may want to prime the pump with a few suggestions, such as:

- Graffiti removal work day (community service)
- Monthly swim parties (outreach)
- Tree planting (community service)
- Convalescent ministry (community service)
- Hosting the pastoral staff for dinner, cooking and serving for their families (church service)
- Trash cleanup at the park or beach (community service)
- Organizing and promoting a special Christian concert (evangelism)
- Church work day (church service)

Let the students take ownership, and include them in a meaningful way through the brainstorming process. If you are going to ask them for their input, be sure to listen! Nothing will discourage your students more than having their voices ignored *after* you have asked them to share.

Remember: In brainstorming, all ideas are written down (I suggest a whiteboard) and are not critiqued during the process. Following the brainstorming process, ask the students to vote for their top three choices for each category. I recommend this be done anonymously, on slips of paper, to avoid peer pressure and hurt feelings.

7:00-8:00 p.m. Teaching #2: Qualities of a Great Leader (Nehemiah 1-6)

Open this study with a statement like, "Perhaps one of the greatest leaders in the Bible, Nehemiah, personifies the qualities that everyone would like to possess. Tonight we will look closely at the ingredients of great leadership with a character sketch of Nehemiah."

Do not read all six chapters in this study. The students should already be familiar with the first two chapters from their quiet time. Make yourself familiar with the whole book of Nehemiah ahead of time so that you can help piece together the account of the rebuilding of the walls of Jerusalem.

Start a discussion about leadership qualities related to the Nehemiah account by using the following eleven statements and reading the related passages. Follow each statement by asking the group if there is anything else they see in the passage you are discussing that relates to your point. For example: "Is there anything else you see in this passage that speaks to the issue of strong leadership?"

A great leader **feels and hurts** (1:4)

A great leader **fasts and prays** for his or her community (1:4)

A great leader is **bold** (2:4-5)

A great leader has a **heart for God** and **love for the people** he or she leads (2:12)

A great leader has **help** (2:17-18)

A great leader is **confident in God** (2:19-20)

A great leader **knows names** (chapter 3)

A great leader **produces courage** for his or her community (4:7-15)

A great leader is **sensitive to others' needs** (chapter 5)

A great leader is usually **opposed by ungodly people** (6:1-2)

A great leader is **obedient in spite of opposition** (6:3-9)

Next, lead a time of reflection and discussion, using the following questions:

How does the story of Nehemiah encourage you?

Which of the eleven qualities of Nehemiah's leadership do you have? What three qualities would you like to grow stronger in?

Which issues in your school and community are important enough to you to cause you to weep, mourn, pray, and fast?

What does the Lord want you to accomplish in <u>your</u> community?

Who and what do you need to accomplish what the Lord is calling you to do?

What one of the eleven qualities do you most want to develop in your life?

8:00-9:00 p.m. Concert of prayer

Break your students into twos and threes. Give your students a focus for their prayer (e.g., a particular high school or city) and encourage each group of students to pray short and direct prayers for your given subject. Suggested subjects for prayer can include:

• Local cities and towns

• High, junior high, and middle schools

• Specific teachers, coaches, and school administrators

• Local athletic teams

• Local churches

- The community as a whole
- Specific saved and unsaved friends
- Campus ministries

9:30-10:00 p.m. Faith Walk: The Steps of Faith

When you've finished your prayer time, explain that it's time for a Faith Walk. Leave a map of the walk with your adult leaders, then leave the cabin and go to the *end* of the journey. After about five minutes, have your adult leaders send the students out of the cabin one at a time, approximately thirty seconds apart, with no flashlights. Each student walks through the darkness, according to the instructions they were given, until they reach you. (Have all of the students that have completed the walk wait with you until the last person arrives.) Most kids find this to be a challenging exercise, with some crying, some nervously singing praise songs, and others silently stoic as they take the Faith Walk. After everyone has completed the walk, return to the cabin and debrief. The following questions can help to open this time:

What did you think about on your walk?
What did you learn about yourself?
Why do you think we did this faith walk?

After the discussion is finished, read Psalm 23. Remind them that godly leadership is often like "walking through the valley of the shadow of death." A slogan we like to quote in our student leadership team is, "What's right isn't always popular, and what's popular isn't always right."

Allow time for students to share their reactions to the walk, and the concept of courage in leadership. Close in prayer, and then move on to dessert!

9:00-10:00 a.m. Quiet time

Have students read Joshua 24. When they have finished, they should answer the following questions in their notebooks:

> What qualities of leadership does Joshua demonstrate in this chapter? (Name at least three.)
>
> Why do you think Joshua gives the people a history lesson at the beginning of the chapter?
>
> What happens after Joshua dies? Do the people continue to serve the Lord, or do they fall away? What do you think this says about Joshua?
>
> Do you think Joshua was obedient to God's call on his life in Joshua 1:9? Why or why not?

10:00-11:00 a.m. Testimonies, sharing, and group prayer

This is a critical time in the retreat, when students are asked to communicate what the Lord has done *in* them and *for* them. It is a time to make a commitment to act on what God has shown them.

Have your students make an altar in the woods nearby (using sticks, rocks, and whatever else they can find) to remember what God has prompted them to do and what they learned from the weekend. After the altar is built, lead a time of testimony and sharing. Encourage kids to share specifically as to what they have dedicated to the Lord in service. Intersperse the testimonies with worship songs and verses such as Genesis 12:7 and 13:18. Conclude with a time of one-sentence prayers as individual students declare their commitment to serve God in leadership.

Youth In Action Application

Write your answers on separate sheets of paper and attach them to this application.

1. Why do you want to be involved in student leadership?

2. What strengths and weaknesses do you feel you would bring to Youth in Action?

3. Describe a situation in which you have stood up for your faith.

4. Name two people who have significantly impacted your life, and tell how they made a difference.

5. What is something God is doing in your life right now?

6. Describe how you came to know Jesus as your personal Lord and Savior.

7. Ask a question we haven't asked, and then answer it.

8. Write a letter to a friend who isn't a Christian in which you share the Gospel.

9. Are you available one hour before youth group for training?

10. Please list three references we may contact regarding your character:

    1. Peer reference
    Name _____

    Address _____

    City_____ Phone_____

    2. Adult reference
    Name _____

    Address _____

    City_____ Phone_____

    3. Pastoral/ministry reference
    Name _____

    Address _____

    City_____ Phone_____

SHANTYTOWN

Mike DeVries

THE BIG IDEA

This retreat is designed to prepare your youth group to effectively minister to the homeless, or in a cross-cultural setting. This experience will give your students a better understanding of what it actually feels like to live on the street. (This retreat works best when paired up with an upcoming outreach to an inner-city neighborhood or cross-cultural environment.)

WHO SHOULD ATTEND

High school and/or junior high school students who will be involved in upcoming inner-city ministry or who want to develop their compassion for the homeless through experiencing one night of what the homeless experience daily.

LOCATION

A large open area, possibly your church parking lot or a basketball court. You will also need a nearby hall or room to serve as your "mission."

TIME FRAME

5:00 p.m. Friday to noon Saturday

WHAT TO BRING

✓ Sleeping bags
✓ Warm clothes
✓ Bible
✓ Notebook
✓ Pen or pencil

NECESSARY INGREDIENTS

★ Cardboard boxes (various sizes)
★ 55-gallon drums to build fires in
    (or metal trash cans)
★ Dinner items (canned beans, canned soup, bread,
    water, etc.)
★ Blankets

(continued)

NECESSARY INGREDIENTS

★ Props/decorations (street signs, "graffiti" banners, store-front posters or banners, city skyline banner, trash to scatter around, newspapers)
★ B.B.Q.-type screens to lay over 55-gallon drums for cooking
★ Scrap wood for cooking fires
★ Matches and lighter fluid
★ Minimal cooking utensils (e.g., one can opener, one ladle, spoons)
★ "Vouchers" for beds at the "mission" (optional)
★ A hall or room to be your "mission"
★ Mattresses for your "mission" beds (optional)
★ Items for "mission-style" breakfast (eggs, toast, stewed prunes, juice, black coffee)
★ Camera and film for team picture

SCHEDULE

FRIDAY

5:00 p.m.	Parents/sponsors meet for instructions
6:00 p.m.	Students arrive and meet at designated area
6:15 p.m.	Orientation and explanation
6:30 p.m.	Search #1: Shelter
8:15 p.m.	Sharing and orientation for Search #2
8:30 p.m.	Search #2: Food and vouchers
9:00 p.m.	Dinner (food found or from the mission)
9:30 p.m.	Evening session
10:30 p.m.	Bedtime ("missionaries" hand out blankets)
11:00 p.m.	Lights out

SATURDAY

7:00 a.m.	Doors open for "mission" and breakfast is served
8:00 a.m.	Morning session
10:00 a.m.	Team picture
10:30 a.m.	Cleanup (be sure to dispose of "shantytown" litter properly)
11:30 a.m.	Departure

RETREAT COMPONENTS

5:00-6:00 p.m. Parents/sponsors meet for instructions

Go over the purpose and the evening in detail. Answer any questions they may have. Be attentive to parental concerns. Go over any individual responsibilities. Spend some time in prayer for the evening.

6:00-6:15 p.m. Students arrive and meet at designated area

Keep outside any items the students will need. Lock away any items that will take away from the experience.

6:15-6:30 p.m. Orientation and explanation

Explain the evening and purpose. Be sure to set the tone with the students right away. This is to be "fun," but it also to be used as an experience to help them better understand homeless people. They should take this evening seriously. Answer any questions they may have. Explain Search #1. Spend some time in prayer.

6:30-8:15 p.m. Search #1: Shelter

Have the group split into smaller groups with at least one adult volunteer per group. Set clear boundaries for the search. Send the groups out to look for items to build a homeless "shantytown"—cardboard, wood, sheets, blankets, tarpaulins, etc. Anything they can beg for, forage, or obtain is legal, but they cannot go to someone they know and ask for items. While they are out on the search, put out the 55-gallon drums, trash, newspapers, posters, and banners. Also, hide the food and cooking utensils around the church area or local vicinity. When your students and adults return, give them time to build their "shantytown" as well as to light fires in the 55-gallon drums (have an adult supervise the lighting).

8:15-8:30 p.m. Sharing and orientation for Search #2

Have your kids share how they felt begging for something to sleep in for the night. How do they think homeless people feel doing this in real life? Have them share any other feelings and thoughts about the experience.

8:30-9:00 p.m. Search #2: Food and vouchers

Explain to your students that there are several cans of food hidden throughout the church property. If they find them, they have found dinner. If not, they'll need to borrow or beg for their dinner. Give your students the boundaries for the search, then set them loose. During the search, have a "missionary," in front of everyone, take one student out to a nearby fast-food restaurant for dinner.

9:00-9:30 p.m. Dinner

Eat the found food by heating up the cans on your 55-gallon-drum B.B.Q.s, then eat out of the cans with spoons. Challenge the students to keep complaining to a minimum.

9:30-10:30 p.m. Evening session

Lead a debrief from Search #2. Have your kids share how it felt to rummage for food and to see someone else get asked to go to dinner. Spend time in worship and singing. Then share the following message:

The Heart and Ministry of Jesus

Read Philippians 2:5-8 and John 12:26. We need to be the hands and feet of God. To do that, we need to act and react as Jesus would respond. Ask, "What would Jesus think of our trip? What would Jesus do on our trip?"

Help your kids to try to picture Jesus in action. What would he do in the city?

Now read Mark 1:40-42. Then read the background on leprosy (Leviticus 13:45-46).

Jesus demonstrated:
    A. Compassion
        • Jesus had compassion on the man
        • It's a heart attitude
        • It's feeling your pain in my heart

    B. Concern
        • He reached out to an "outsider"
        • He reached out to an unnoticed person
        • We need to reach out to those who people tend to forget or ignore

    C. Courage
        • Jesus touched the "untouchable"
        • Why did he touch?
                *To identify with the man
                *To show unconditional love to the man
        • He did more than just notice the man, he touched him . . . ministry

What about us?
    A. Compassion
        • Read Matthew 9:36
        • We need to be willing to have our hearts broken with what breaks
            God's heart

    B. Prayer
        • Ask God to allow us to see and feel as he does
        • Ask God to break our hearts
        • Ask God to meet us in the city

    C. Power
        • Be willing to allow God to use us
        • Leave the results to him
        • The Holy Spirit will be faithful to do God's work through us
            (see Philippians 1:6)
        • Allow God to work: React to him

Have your kids share how they feel their "shantytown" experience relates to the life of the homeless in the city, their upcoming ministry to the homeless, or what it must be like to be homeless. End in prayer or more worship.

10:30 p.m. Bedtime
Have your "missionaries" come and hand out blankets to your students, and possibly offer them a little food.

SATURDAY

7:00-8:00 a.m. Doors open for "mission" and breakfast is served
Your students will invariably wake up before the "mission" is open. Make them stand in a line outside the door of the "mission." If students get out of hand, send them to the end of the line, or kick them out of line permanently (to go find their own food). At around 7:30, open the doors and start breakfast. Have students form a line and pass by your servers. Have your servers give limited portions until everyone has some (students will complain, but so do the homeless). Offer seconds only after everyone has been served. Don't be afraid to run out of food, as some missions often do.

8:00-10:00 a.m. Morning session
Begin with worship, then debrief the entire experience. Have your kids share

their feelings about the experience. What impacted them the most? How has this experience changed their view of the homeless? How will it affect their upcoming ministry in the city?

When you've finished your debrief, take a good hour to an hour-and-a-half to go over the logistics for your upcoming mission trip in detail. End your time with prayer and two to three worship choruses like "Awesome God," "Servant of All," and "I Love You, Lord."

AUTHOR'S NOTES

The key to making this retreat unforgettable is to make the experience as realistic as possible. The more lifelike the experience, the more culturally sensitive your students will become. The incredible thing about this experience is to watch the interaction between the students: to see their emotions, struggles, and frustrations as they experience a piece of hopelessness. We have seen students lash out at other students who got something they didn't get. Some students become selfish; others show remarkable compassion toward their fellow "homeless." Students grapple with all the frustration and hopelessness that goes with homelessness. In the end, they come out changed, equipped with compassion and understanding for the homeless they are soon to minister to.

CREATIVE OPTIONS
- Decorate the area you will be using with extra 55-gallon drums (complete with fire), trash, newspapers, wooden palettes, posters, and banners.
- Visit and tour a rescue mission before your retreat. Find out as much as you can about the workings of the mission and about the people they serve. Tell them what you are planning and ask for input to make the experience more realistic. Take some of your "missionaries" with you to serve at the mission to get a feel for their role in your simulation experience.
- Include a police officer in this experience. Often the police are called upon to remove homeless individuals from certain locations. Have your police officer come in the middle of the night and "move" some of your "homeless" students from their "home."
- Don't tell your students ahead of time that they will be spending the night in a "shantytown." Surprise them when it comes time to go to bed.
- Limit the amount of cookware and utensils. Make your students borrow, barter, or steal cookware and utensils.
- Use mission "vouchers." During Search #1, hide pieces of paper that say *Mission Voucher* on them. During Search #2, anyone who finds a voucher can trade it in at the "mission" for a mattress indoors for the night. Vouchers can also be traded for food and other items they might need (blankets, shelter, cooking utensils, etc.).

Girls' Absolute Blast

Kara Eckmann

THE BIG IDEA

This retreat provides an opportunity for high school or junior high girls to get together at a local home for a night of teaching directed at some of the issues young women face, and the chance to discover God's plan for their lives. Teenage girls and teenage guys are different. Each gender needs the chance to spend "safe" time together. A strategic youth ministry will include all-girls and all-guys retreats into their calendar. We have two Girls Absolute Blast overnighters a year: one in the spring and one during the summer break.

WHO SHOULD ATTEND

High school *or* junior high girls (do not mix).

LOCATION

A local home large enough to handle the group.

TIME FRAME

Twenty-four hours, Friday night through Saturday night

WHAT TO BRING

- ✓ Sleeping bag
- ✓ Toiletries
- ✓ Bible
- ✓ Pen or pencil
- ✓ Notebook

NECESSARY INGREDIENTS

- ★ Food for two meals (one breakfast and one lunch)
- ★ Snack food for break times (have the girls bring their favorite snacks and set up a snack table)
- ★ Name tags
- ★ Video, TV monitor, and VCR
- ★ Handouts of the theme for each girl (make sure the handouts have plenty of writing space)
- ★ Board games
- ★ Craft materials
- ★ Prizes

SCHEDULE

[**Note:** All participants to eat dinner before arriving at church]

7:00 p.m.	Meet at church
7:15 p.m.	Leave church; drive to nearby home
7:30 p.m.	Welcome and orientation
7:40 p.m.	Common Bond
7:50 p.m.	Session I: Getting Below the Surface
8:20 p.m.	Small groups
8:50 p.m.	Break
9:15 p.m.	Session II: Our Friendships with Guys
10:15 p.m.	Break
12:00 a.m.	Put on movie; folks start going to bed
2:00 a.m.	Bedtime (hopefully)

8:00 a.m.	Rise and shine!
8:30 a.m.	Breakfast
9:15 a.m.	Small groups
9:45 a.m.	Session III: Our Friendships with Each Other
10:15 a.m.	Break
10:30 a.m.	Session IV: Our Friendship with God
11:15 a.m.	Small groups
11:45 a.m.	Large group sharing and prayer
12:15 p.m.	Lunch
1:00 p.m.	Free time
4:00 p.m.	Start cleaning the house
5:00 p.m.	Meet the guys for dinner (if they have been having their own retreat at another location)
7:00 p.m.	Back at church

RETREAT COMPONENTS

FRIDAY

7:40-7:50 p.m. Common Bond

Have the girls get into threesomes. Have them interview one another and see which group can come up with the most things that all three girls have in common (e.g., we all have brown hair, our fathers are all named Tom, we were all born in Michigan, etc.)

7:50-8:20 p.m. Session I: Getting Below the Surface

Teenage girls are notorious for huddling in cliques and excluding outsiders. This session is effective only if your speaker is unknown to the group. Ask her to dress in a sloppy manner, wear little make-up, and have messy hair. In other words, ask her to come as a nerd (and have her introduce herself with an unpopular name). She should try to blend in with the group from the time your group meets at the church until Session I. Chances are that your students will ignore her and possibly even make fun of her, or maybe your students will reach out to her and accept her. Either way, this will be a lesson they will never forget about accepting other people as you introduce your special guest speaker and up walks "the nerd."

Ask your students the following questions:
   "What did you think when you first saw her?"
   "How do you feel now that you know that she is not a "nerd," but our
      speaker?"

Ask your speaker the following questions:
   "How did you feel when you walked into this group?"
   "Did people make you feel welcome?"

Then, have your speaker share from 1 Samuel 16:7 and describe how she felt when people judged her by her outward appearances. Her reactions could include:
   Feelings of being dehumanized, like an object
   Humiliation
   Pressure to conform to the expectations of the group
   Anger at being compared to others and not being accepted for oneself

When the speaker has finished sharing, have her ask the girls if they are able to relate to these responses as well. Allow for any sharing if time permits.

8:20-8:50 p.m. Small groups

Capitalize on your overnite as a time for adult volunteers to build relationships with your girls. Use your adults as small group leaders. Ask them ahead of time who they want in their small groups so they can be strategically matched. Encourage them to view free time as a chance to build relationships.

In your small groups, discuss the following questions:
"When have you felt judged by how you look?"
"Why do we so often judge people by their appearances?"
"How does that affect our chances of making new friends?"

9:15-10:15 p.m. Session II: Our Friendships with Guys

Girls are consumed with wanting to know about the opposite gender. In this smaller setting, they may be more open to asking honest questions. Arrange ahead of time for two high school guys and one college-age or adult guy to share on a special panel. Have your guest speaker moderate the panel. Include the following questions:

- What are you looking for in a friendship with a girl?
- How is friendship with a girl different than if you want to date her?
- What confuses you about girls?
- How do you feel when you ask a girl out?
- What is your opinion about girls asking guys out on a date?
- Does the guy need to pay for the date? If so, why? If not, why not?
- What is the kindest way to break up with a guy?
- Can girls and guys just be friends?

Along with the above questions, take questions from the girls themselves. After the panel discussion, ask your guest speaker to share the ABCDs of healthy dating relationships:

Acceptance
Do you feel accepted by the other person?
Do you feel pressured to conform to a certain image or standard?
Do you accept the other person the way you want to be accepted?

Boundaries
Do you both understand how far is too far sexually?
How well do you give each other "space" when you need it?
Are you able to comfortably ask for and respect the need for privacy?
Can you communicate to the other comfortably when you feel your boundaries have been violated?

Communication
Can you talk about subjects that interest both of you?

Can you talk about things that are only of interest to one of you?
Can you disagree without fighting?
Can you have an argument and make up afterward?

Devotions
Can you pray together?
Can you read the Bible and study it together?
Are you spiritually compatible?
Do you worship the same God?

10:15 p.m.-12:00 a.m. Break

You can do quite a lot of things with this break time—play board games, swim if there's a pool, and do crafts like decorating plastic drink glasses or plastic visors and making friendship bracelets or necklaces.

12:00-2:00 a.m. Video

Take care choosing the video to show to your group. You don't want to contradict what you are teaching them by showing a movie that has inappropriate content. Try a classic that all the girls would enjoy, like *The Sound of Music*, *The Wizard of Oz*, *Casablanca*, etc.

9:15-9:45 a.m. Small groups

This is a time for fun, yet meaningful small-group competition. Break your girls into small groups with at least one adult in each small group. Then have the groups compete to come up with the best submission for an assignment you give them. Assignment ideas can include:

- Make a Top Ten List of Friendship Killers
- Make a Top Ten List of Friendship Builders
- Create and perform a three-minute skit that demonstrates at least four of the friendship qualities mentioned in 1 Corinthians 13

When all the groups are ready, have each group read their list aloud and/or perform their skit for the rest of the group. Award prizes to the winning group.

9:45-10:15 a.m. Session III: Our Friendships with Each Other

Begin by having the girls share from their Top Ten Lists. Then, have the speaker share from Philippians 2:1-4, bringing out the following points:

> ***We must put others first (striving for unity in diversity).***
> What are some simple steps we can take to put others first?
> How can we develop an "other-orientation" instead of a "me-orientation?"
> Read Matthew 5:46-47. What does Jesus tell us about loving others in these verses?
>
> ***We must put ourselves last ("me last" instead of "me first").***
> How do we put ourselves last?
> What does someone who is truly humble look like?
> According to Proverbs 3:34, what does God do for the humble? (See also Luke 14:7-14.)
> How does putting ourselves last promote friendships?

When the speaker has finished, follow up by asking, "What does Philippians 2:1-4 tell us about our friendships with each other?"

10:30-11:15 a.m. Session IV: Our Friendship with God

Our most important friendship is our relationship with God. At the heart of this friendship is love.

Have your speaker read Luke 15:11-24 in the form of a melodrama. As she reads each verse or passage, have volunteers from your group act out, whether in mime or skit form, what Jesus is describing in this parable of the prodigal son. When the melodrama is finished, ask, "How do we see God's love in the prodigal son parable?"

Draw out the following answers:

1. God's love is *unbreakable,* even when the son turned his back on his dad (see also Romans 8:38-39).

2. God's love is *unconditional*—Dad comes running out to his son with open arms. We don't have to get our act together; God loves us no matter what we do.

3. God's love is *unimaginable.* Ask the girls to identify some things they love (e.g., ice cream, boys, TV, the beach, etc.). Explain how the parable of the prodigal son shows how God's love is way beyond our love for things or other people.

11:15-11:45 a.m. Small groups
Break into small groups with at least one adult in each small group. Have the adult lead a discussion using the following questions:

"How is our friendship with God different than our friendship with other people?"

"How can we cultivate our friendship with God?"

"What are the things that get in the way of our friendship with God?"

"How can we deal with those obstacles?"

11:45 a.m-12:15 p.m. Large group sharing and prayer
Encourage several girls to share what stands out about the weekend so far. Allow time for as many girls to share as possible. After several girls have shared, gather in a circle and hold hands. Lead a time of group prayer, asking God to continue to teach us to have better friendships with guys, with each other, and with him.

YOU'RE IN HIS ARMY NOW

Frank Riley & Tony Allmonslecher

THE BIG IDEA

This retreat, based on an infantry theme, teaches junior high (and possibly young high school) students to serve the Commander faithfully, recognize the Enemy, and follow their specific mission assignments.

This retreat is designed to give students a vision for their local community and provide them with practical and spiritual tools to accomplish great things for God.

In his letter to Timothy, Paul instructs his young friend to be a good soldier for Christ (2 Timothy 2:3). This retreat gives students the basic training that every "soldier" needs. Everything for the weekend is in military lingo—free time is *liberty*, organized recreation is *maneuvers*, and the talent show is the *USO Show*.

WHO SHOULD ATTEND

Junior high and possibly young high school students. The retreat works best with at least sixteen students and no more than forty.

LOCATION

Either a conference center or cabin; if the group is over twenty students, we recommend a conference center.

TIME FRAME

Friday evening to Sunday afternoon

WHAT TO BRING

✓ Sleeping bags   ✓ Toiletries
✓ Flashlights   ✓ Bible
✓ Notebook   ✓ Pen or pencil

NECESSARY INGREDIENTS

★ T-shirt
★ Training manual (notes and retreat schedule) for each student
★ Copies of youth devotional for every student (see page 91)
★ "Dog tags" (name tags) for each student
★ Grape juice and bread for communion

(continued)

★ "Mission Orders" packet for each "platoon"
★ Tape of military band marches
★ A *Christian Flag* (A Christian flag is a white flag with a blue area in the upper left corner with a white cross in it. It also has gold fringe around the edges. Many Christian bookstores carry this flag or it can be ordered through Carrott Top Industries at 1-800-628-3524.)
★ Video camera and blank videocassettes
★ TV monitor and VCR
★ Videos (e.g., *Red Dawn*, *Predator*, *Rambo*)
★ Markers
★ Whiteboard or butcher paper
★ Clothesline and enough clothespins for each student
★ Snack food

SCHEDULE

FRIDAY

[**Note:** All participants to eat dinner before arriving at church]
1730 (5:30 p.m.) Meet at church load vehicles
1830 (6:30 p.m.) Leave church
2000 (8:00 p.m.) Arrive at camp and settle into "barracks" (cabins)
2015 (8:15 p.m.) Snack in the "mess hall" (dining hall)
2100 (9:00 p.m.) Session #1: Recognizing the Enemy
2145 (9:45 p.m.) Platoons
2230 (10:30 p.m.) Activity
2330 (11:30 p.m.) "Taps" (lights out)

SATURDAY

0700 (7:00 a.m.) Reveille and morning watch
0800 (8:00 a.m.) Breakfast
0915 (9:15 a.m.) Session #2: Basic Training
1015 (10:15 a.m.) Platoons

1200 (12:00 p.m.) Lunch
1300 (1:00 p.m.) "Liberty" (free time)
1600 (4:00 p.m.) "Maneuvers" (all-group games)
1800 (6:00 p.m.) Dinner
1830 (6:30 p.m.) Staff meeting
1915 (7:15 p.m.) Session #3: Victory in Christ
2025 (8:25 p.m.) Final platoon meeting
2130 (9:30 p.m.) "USO Show" (talent show)
2400 (12:00 a.m.) Taps

SUNDAY

0700 (7:00 a.m.) Reveille and morning watch
0800 (8:00 a.m.) Morning worship and platoon sharing
1030 (10:30 a.m.) Brunch
1115 (11:15 a.m.) Clean up and pack up

RETREAT COMPONENTS

FRIDAY

1730-1830 (5:30-6:30 p.m.) Meet at church, load vehicles

This retreat begins at the "Troop Depot" (church). As students register (and are inducted into God's Army) they should be greeted by adults in military clothing. These adults then take care of the following:

> Issue *Training Manual* (notes and retreat schedule)
> Conduct *weapon check* (did they bring a Bible?)
> Issue *dog tag* (name tag)
> Conduct *inspection* (check registration form, permission slip, money, etc.)

Loading vehicles should be supervised by "drill sergeants" who, instead of yelling obscenities, are screaming encouragements!

The place is booming with a tape of military band marches borrowed from a local band director or purchased at a local music store.

2000-2045 (8:00-8:45 p.m.) Arrive at camp and settle into barracks

Have students disembark from vehicles one-quarter to one-half mile from camp. Form them into ranks, as drill sergeants move them forward, with Christian cadences. Also, unfurl the Christian flag in front of your troops.

Upon arriving at the barracks, each young person receives a retreat T-shirt with a retreat logo on the back and a private rank stripe on the side sleeve. Each rank is the same because in God's Army everyone is of equal worth.

2100-2145 (9:00-9:45 p.m.) Session #1: Recognizing the Enemy (Ephesians 6:12)

Begin by reading Ephesians 6:12 to your group twice. Follow this with action clips from popular movies such as *Red Dawn, Predator,* or any of Sylvester Stallone's *Rambo* films, as illustrations of the need to understand and recognize the enemy's strategy. (*Predator* makes a good illustration because the enemy is invisible.)

[**WARNING:** These videos contain language and other situations that you may feel are inappropriate for your group. Carefully screen any clips before you show them, and show only clips that you are satisfied are appropriate, or substitute another video or activity here.]

Next, read Nehemiah 6:1-3, highlighting the importance of *recognizing the enemy* as those who seek to keep us from what God has called us to do in his name. Ask the following question: "What do you think God wants you to do specifically that the enemy is or will try to prevent you from doing?" Break your students into twos or threes and have them share their answers with one another. Allow about five minutes for this interaction.

When your sharing time has finished, bring your students back together. Give kids a chance to share their answers with the whole group. Then ask, "If *you* were the Devil, what would you do to keep Christian students from living effective Christian lives?" Record their answers on a whiteboard or butcher paper. Possible answers could include:
- Tempt Christians to indulge in drugs and alcohol at parties
- Convince Christians that church isn't important
- Make Christians afraid to speak out about Jesus on their campuses
- Get Christians to believe that sex outside of marriage is all right if you love the person

Now, help your kids to *understand the battlefield.* Explain that the battlefield is right where they are—their schools, their homes, their workplaces. Satan is battling for their allegiance, and even their very souls. But even though it is truly a battle, the weapons at our disposal aren't guns, tanks, or bombs. The battle is fought with prayer!

Next, write the following verses on your whiteboard or butcher paper:
Romans 12:1-2
Ephesians 6:18-20
Romans 15:30
Romans 16:20

Have student volunteers look up and read each of these Scriptures aloud. Then have all your students look them up and read them individually. After they have finished, stand and sing one or two worship songs that relate directly to spiritual warfare, such as "The Battle Belongs to the Lord" and "Bind us Together," with everyone holding hands.

2145-2230 (9:45-10:30 p.m.) Platoons

Break your students into approximately five small "platoons" with at least one adult leader per platoon. Each platoon is given a packet marked TOP SECRET. The packet contains their mission orders.

Each small group now uses this time to open their "orders" and plan the mission they have been given. On Sunday morning, each group will share their mission with the larger group, and will be encouraged to carry out their mission upon returning home. Challenge them to include all necessary details, such as plan of attack, timetables, supplies needed, etc. They must plan allowing for the fact that Satan will try to thwart their endeavor each step of the way.

Here are some examples of "missions" you can give your platoons.

MISSION TO YOUR SCHOOLS

Your mission is to evangelize your campus! Think of as many ways as possible to accomplish this task. Answering the following questions can help you get started:

1. Who are the individual "groups" on our campuses (e.g., jocks, druggies, etc.)?
2. How many Christians are on our campuses?
3. Who are the Christian teachers and administrators on our campuses?
4. What is Jesus Christ's attitude toward our schoolmates?
5. How are we as modern-day Christians called to treat our schoolmates?
6. How can we show Christ in our lives on our campuses?
7. What ways can we share Christ with our schoolmates?

MISSION TO THE ELDERLY

Look around your town. On almost any street, you can find people over sixty-five years of age. Your mission will be to plan and implement an outreach to people in your community who are over sixty-five years old. Answering the following questions can help you get started:

1. Where are elderly people located in our area?
2. How many do we personally know?
3. What are some special needs that elderly people might have?
4. Are there certain groups of elderly people we could concentrate on ministering to?
5. What will such a ministry require?
6. What will it cost?
7. How much time will it take?
8. Will our ministry be a one-time "commando raid" or a longer campaign?
9. What will we do? When will we do it? Who will be responsible? What special resources will we need?

MISSION TO YOUR COMMUNITY

Your mission: to impact your community for Christ! Answering the following questions can help you get started:

1. What are the needs of our community (e.g., homeless/hungry, new immigrants, gangs, animals, environmental, litter, graffiti, etc.)?
2. What problems need to be addressed that relate to those needs (e.g., language barriers for immigrants, no sense of belonging for street kids, finding jobs for the homeless, etc.)?
3. What area of need can we focus on?

4. How can our efforts bring Christ into our community?
5. What will we set as our specific goals (e.g., adopt an immigrant family, run a "Clean the City" week, etc.)?
6. What steps will be required? Who will be responsible to implement them?
7. What resources will we need to accomplish our mission (e.g., money, outside help, newspaper coverage, place to hold event, equipment, garbage bags, shoestrings, etc.)?
8. What is our timetable? When will we carry out our plan?

MISSION TO THE FAMILY

You have one of the toughest missions—serving your families! What can you do to impact them for Christ? Answering the following questions will help you get started:

1. What problems do many of our families face (e.g., divorce, brother-sister arguments, money, etc.)?
2. How can we help bring our families closer together in Christ (e.g., church-sponsored events and outings, youth group-sponsored events, parent-teen dialogue sessions, etc.)?
3. How can we provide support for our youth group families (e.g., youth group families' dinner, parents' group, etc.)?
4. What specific plans of action do we want to take?
5. What steps will be required?
6. Who will handle each step?
7. What resources will we need to accomplish our mission?
8. Where will we obtain those resources?
9. What is our mission timetable?

In addition to each platoon's mission, give each platoon an extra order to create a five-minute skit based on the retreat theme, "You're in His Army Now," that will be performed at the "USO Show" on Saturday night.

2230-2330 (10:30-11:30 p.m.) Activity

Here are two options. First, "Capture the Flag" is great to play if you have enough room, flashlights, and visibility. The game is consistent with the weekend theme. The other possibility is for your students to break into groups of four or five and "interrogate" each other. One person at a time will each be interviewed by the group for approximately eight minutes. At that time, announce that once this current question is answered, the group must "interrogate" the next person. This goes on until everyone has been interviewed. You may wish to give them some possible questions to spark their creativity such as:

"What makes you happy as a Christian?"
"Other than Jesus, who do you admire the most in the Bible, and why?"
"What would you like to have written on your tombstone?"

2330 (11:30 p.m.) Taps (lights out)

Close each evening with "Taps," either from a recording or live, if you have a trumpet or bugle player in your group.

SATURDAY

0700-0800 (7:00-8:00 a.m.) Reveille and morning watch

Start the morning with "Reveille," either from a recording or live, if you have a trumpet or bugle player in your group.

For "morning watch" (quiet time), supply your students with copies of a quality teen devotional. We recommend any of the devotional guides by Jim Burns: *Spirit Wings* (Vine Books), *Getting in Touch With God* (Harvest House), or *90 Days Through The New Testament* (Regal Books).

0800-0850 (8:00-8:50 a.m.) Breakfast

Being an army means working together for one another's survival. String clothespins on a line strung across mess hall. Each kid will have a pin with his or her name on it. Tell your students to take time during the weekend to pin notes of encouragement to other students. Keep your eyes on the clothespins and make sure that every student gets at least one note of encouragement.

0915-1015 (9:15-10:15 a.m.) Session #2: Basic Training

Open by reading 1 Corinthians 9:24-27 out loud to the group. Relate the story of Ben Johnson, the Canadian sprinter who apparently had won the 1988 Olympic gold medal in the 100-meter sprint, only to be disqualified for steroid usage. Ask, "What could disqualify you from being an effective witness for Jesus?" (For example, cheating on tests, drinking, cursing, etc.) Solicit answers from your students and record these on a whiteboard.

Next, have your students break into twos or threes. Read 2 Timothy 2:1-5 to the students. Direct the small groups to review the list of life issues found in this passage that hinder the credibility of their faith, and identify one or more of these which they struggle with. Have them share their findings together, followed by a short time of prayer for one another.

When the time of prayer is over, bring the group back together and read Hebrews 12:1-3, challenging your students to put off the things of the world, and to put on the full armor of God. Lead a discussion where your kids can brainstorm practical ways that they can build this scriptural advice into their daily lives.

Close this time in a victory song such as "Our God Reigns" or "Awesome God."

1015-1130 (10:15-11:30 a.m.) Platoons

Have your students break into their platoons. Give them time to continue to work on their mission strategies, reminding them to have them ready to share on Sunday morning. Stop in and spend time with each platoon, answering questions and providing suggestions to keep them on track. Make sure they take time to work on their five-minute skit for the USO Show on Saturday night.

1300-1600 (1:00-4:00 p.m.) Liberty

Provide a variety of free time options, including team sports, a board game room, etc. Also, encourage your "Drill Instructors" (counselors) to spend some one-on-one time with their students.

1600-1730 (4:00-5:30 p.m.) Maneuvers

Get your students and adults together out on a big field. Run some all-group team games like Capture the Flag and Ultimate Frisbee.

1915-2025 (7:15-8:25 p.m.) Session #3: Victory in Christ

Begin by having three student volunteers read Romans 16:20, 1 John 4:4, and Romans 8:37-39 aloud to the group. Ask, "What do these verses tell us about spiritual warfare? How do these verses encourage us as we face the reality of spiritual warfare?" Allow for sharing and record their answers on a whiteboard or butcher paper.

Next, read Revelation 12:10-11. Ask, "Why is 'The word of our testimony' so important and helpful in achieving our victory in Christ?" Allow for sharing and record their answers on a whiteboard or butcher paper.

Now have each student write their personal Christian testimonies. Encourage them to keep three points in mind as they write:
> What God *has done* in my life
> What God *is doing* in my life
> What I believe God *will do* in my life

Allow fifteen minutes for your students to complete their testimonies. When everyone is finished, invite willing students to share their testimonies with the group. Begin the sharing with your testimony to help break the ice. (If your group is over twenty-five students, you may want to form two or three small groups to do this exercise.)

When your group has finished sharing, hold a communion service appropriate to the theology and traditions of your group, emphasizing that the power of sin and death has been broken and that our victory is found in the body and blood of our Lord Jesus. (Read Hebrews 4:15-16 and Romans 5:9-11 prior to beginning the communion service.)

Following communion, close with a song like "The Battle Belongs to The Lord."

2025-2130 (8:25-9:30 p.m.) Final platoon meeting
This is the last time the platoons will meet before Sunday morning. Encourage them to focus on putting together their mission strategies. Check in again with each platoon and help them with any further questions or difficulties. Make sure that they're ready for the USO Show coming up next!

2130-2300 (9:30 -11:00 p.m.) USO Show
Open your show with some fun, up-tempo singing, followed by some lively mixer games. Then have each platoon perform their skit for the rest of the group. Videotape your show to play at youth group and use for future promotions.

0700-0800 (7:00-8:00 a.m.) Reveille and morning watch

Have your students continue in their youth devotionals.

0800-1000 (8:00-10:00 a.m.) Morning worship and platoon sharing

Start the morning with some fast songs to wake everyone up and get their attention, then shift into an extended worship time, with lots of praise songs.

When your worship time has finished, have each platoon elect a spokesperson to share its mission strategies with the whole group. Affirm the plans of each platoon, and challenge them to implement their mission strategies when they get home.

Close your time with group prayer. Bring your whole group together in a circle. Have students pray aloud for their missions, asking God to give them the strength and wisdom to fulfill their orders. Close your prayer time with a group hug and an ear-splitting rebel yell!

AUTHORS' NOTE

Follow up with each platoon in the following weeks to help them work out the kinks in their plans and get them started on actually completing their missions.

ROCK 'N WATER

Craig Lomax

THE BIG IDEA

Kids discover—through rock climbing, water rafting and other adventures—how to develop trust in God and God's people. This retreat enables the participants to be the instructors; they teach themselves through the experience.

Time and opportunities are provided for youth and adults to build relationships. The outdoor setting exposes kids to God's creation in new ways. And the element of challenge built into this adventure develops character and self-confidence in youth and adults alike.

WHO SHOULD ATTEND

Everyone! The organization you work with may limit the size of the group, so check first. Ideal group size varies between twelve to thirty-six students and leaders.

LOCATION

You'll want to arrange this trip through an outfitting organization that leads groups through rafting and mountaineering retreat experiences, ideally one that is within a day's drive from your church. These organizations usually offer, for a set fee per person, complete services, including food. Quality outfitting organizations include:

Christian Adventures (Michigan) 616-751-5990
Confrontation Point Ministries (Tennessee) 615-354-3546
Eagle Lake (Colorado) 800-873-2453
Noah's Ark (Colorado) 719-395-2158
Reachout Expeditions (Oregon) 503-234-0704
Reachout Expeditions (Washington) 800-697-3847
Recreation Specialists (California) 800-697-3847
Red Cloud (Colorado) 303-944-2625
Rock 'N Water (California) 916-621-3918
Rocky Mountain High (Colorado) 719-395-2328
Solid Rock (Wyoming) 307-742-7079
Spring Hill Camps/Alpha Expeditions (Michigan)
      616-734-2616
Summit Adventures (California) 800-827-1282

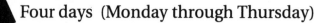

TIME FRAME

Four days (Monday through Thursday)

WHAT TO BRING

✔ Sleeping bag
✔ Wet suit
✔ Hiking shoes/clothes
✔ Sun screen

[**Note:** Check with your outfitter to find out what they already provide and what they recommend that you bring with you.]

NECESSARY INGREDIENTS

★ *Pass It On* cards* (three per student, five per leader)
★ One copy of *The Personal Promise Pocketbook** (Harold Shaw Publishers) for each student
   *Both of these items can be purchased or ordered from a local Christian bookstore.
★ An old volleyball
★ Candle
★ Matches

SCHEDULE

MONDAY

7:00 p.m.	Arrive at base camp, lay out sleeping bags, swim, play random games
8:00 p.m.	Trust Fall
9:00 p.m.	Campfire and orientation
10:30 p.m.	In the sack, under the stars, on the dirt

TUESDAY

7:00 a.m.	Individual devotions
7:30 a.m.	Breakfast
8:00 a.m.	Depart for rock climbing location
9:00 a.m.	Climb, explore, hike, swim, and eat lunch
6:00 p.m.	Dinner at base camp
6:30 p.m.	Free time
8:00 p.m.	Campfire and Teaching #1
10:30 p.m.	In the sack, under the stars, on the dirt

WEDNESDAY

7:30 a.m.	Individual devotions
8:00 a.m.	Breakfast
9:00 a.m.	Whitewater rafting (lunch on river)
4:00 p.m.	Return to camp, dry out
5:00 p.m.	Mountain Ball
6:00 p.m.	Dinner
7:00 p.m.	Free time
8:00 p.m.	Campfire and Teaching #2
9:00 p.m.	Candle Passing
10:30 p.m.	In the sack, under the stars, on the dirt

THURSDAY

7:30 a.m.	Individual devotions
8:00 a.m.	Load gear in vehicles
8:30 a.m.	Breakfast, pray, good-bye!

RETREAT COMPONENTS

MONDAY

8:00 p.m. Trust Fall (minimum of nine people needed)

Have the group form two parallel lines. Evaluate the lines for any weak spots and adjust them accordingly. Each line stands shoulder to shoulder and faces the other line. Each student holds the lower, inside forearm (almost at the wrist) of one partner's left arm and another partner's right. *No arms should be crossed.* This creates a surprisingly strong net.

One person stands on a sturdy box, stool, or other object, elbow to shoulder height, with his or her back squared toward the group and lined up with the line of wrists. Show the group how to bend their knees to absorb impact of the falling person. Instruct the faller to keep his or her hands crossed over the chest (to avoid slapping people) and to keep his or her body straight to spread the weight over the group.

The faller then calls out, "Ready?" When the group collectively responds "Ready!" the faller calls out "Fall!" and falls backwards into the human net. Choose a new faller, rearrange the "net," and continue until everyone has had an opportunity to participate.

[**Note:** Although it is surprising to see how much weight a group can catch with this technique, be careful with this exercise!]

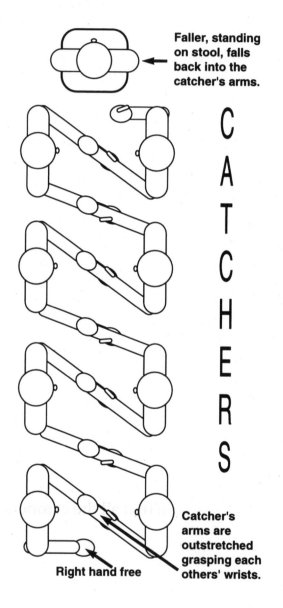

Faller, standing on stool, falls back into the catcher's arms.

C A T C H E R S

Catcher's arms are outstretched grasping each others' wrists.

Right hand free

9:00-10:30 p.m. Campfire and orientation

Following the completion of the Trust Fall, bring the kids back around the campfire. (There is bound to be plenty of excitement and buzzing over their accomplishments—you'll have to speak loudly!) Ask for a few students to share what they learned through the experience. Then ask, "Was it scarier to fall or to catch? Do you trust the people who caught you more now than you did before?"

Follow these questions by reading 1 Samuel 17:19-37, the account of David preparing to fight Goliath. Ask the campers, "According to these verses, where did David gather his confidence to fight Goliath?"

This will dovetail into the orientation for the retreat: "We will learn to trust God more completely in the future as we have successfully trusted him in the past. Just as David was confident against Goliath because of what the Lord had already done for him, so too we can leave camp more confident in the Lord's promises and his character."

At this point, hand out copies of *The Personal Promise Pocketbook* (Harold Shaw Publishers). Explain that the book is divided into three sections:
1. God's promises and purposes for me
2. God's promises and purposes for my relationship with him
3. God's promises and purposes for my relationship with others

This book will serve as a basis for their quiet times, and a reference point throughout the retreat.

Now, hand out three *Pass it On* cards to each person. They are the size of business cards, and each card contains a refreshing Scripture or promise from God's word. The card leaves room for a signature or note from the giver, who then hands it to any member of the camp they want to encourage. That person is encouraged to write their name and "pass it on" to another person. This process can continue throughout the retreat until the card is completely full, and the last person to be handed the card may keep it! (Give extra cards to your adult sponsors and instruct them to make sure that all the campers participate and no one is being left out.)

7:00 a.m. Individual devotions

Have each camper read Section One of *The Personal Promise Pocketbook*, entitled "God's Promises and Purposes for Me."

8:00-10:30 p.m. Campfire and Teaching #1

Open with some fun songs such as "River of Life," "Pharaoh Pharaoh," and "I've Got the Joy," then move into more intimate worship, singing songs like "Only You," "Awesome God," and "Refiner's Fire." Remember, your kids have just been rock climbing and will have been invigorated by their accomplishments. Choose songs that will enhance this time.

When you've finished singing, move into your storytelling time. Open this time by asking, "Who would like to share about something that happened today while we were rock climbing?" You can break the ice by talking about one of the campers you were climbing with—how he or she overcame fear and became a motivator for the group. After some sharing has taken place, segue into a teaching on the nature and character of God. Add your own illustrations and personal examples to enhance the text as you discuss the following seven aspects of the character of God.

Teaching #1: The character of God

We know God by his names and character
1. The Rock (Psalm 92:15)
2. The Strong Tower (Psalm 61:3)
3. An Ever-Present Help (Psalm 46:1)
4. The Deliverer (Psalm 18:2)
5. A Shield (Psalm 3:3)
6. Mighty (Psalm 50:1)
7. A Strong Refuge (Psalm 71:7)

Close the teaching time by drawing analogies between rock climbing and trusting God by knowing his character. Say something like, "Today we learned that God, just like the rope that held us up and didn't break, will never fail. And the rock we climbed was steady and solid, just as the Lord is himself. We can trust him in all things."

Close by singing a song of declaration such as "The Battle Belongs to the Lord," followed by a time of prayer where students are encouraged to pray one-sentence prayers of thanksgiving for God's character and nature. A typical prayer could sound like, "Lord, I thank you that you are my deliverer, and you rescue me."

7:30 a.m. Individual devotions

Have your campers read Section Two of *The Personal Promise Pocketbook,* entitled "God's Promises and Purposes for My Relationship with Him."

5:00-6:00 p.m. Mountain Ball

This is a game that actually has to be experienced to be understood, but here's the idea. Mountain Ball is similar to kick ball, but with no rules or structure. There are two bases instead of three, no base lines, no foul lines (except if the ball gets caught in the trees or floats away on the river), a player can only be tagged out by having the ball touch him or her, and the bases are safe for as many people as can fit.

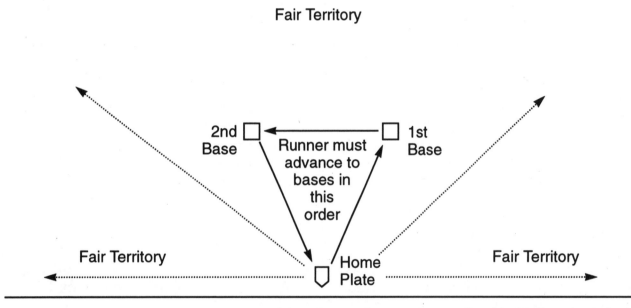

The object of the game goes like this: The pitcher rolls the ball (a kick ball-type of ball or old volley ball) to the kicker at home base. The kicker kicks the ball. The ball is in play as long as the ball is kicked in *any* forward direction. The runner then proceeds to first base. He or she may take as long as he or she likes to get there, and can run anywhere along the way, including into the woods or the river, to avoid being hit by the ball and tagged out. First and second base are "safe" as long as the runner is touching it for the first time. Once the runner's foot leaves a base for any reason, he or she must advance to the next base or run the risk of being tagged out. This means that overrunning a base, sliding into a base, or taking one's foot off of a base are all no-nos. Runners may proceed to second base, and then home, using any route they choose, at any time. Correspondingly, the pitcher and fielders can attempt to hit a runner with the ball (thus "tagging" them out) anytime they can catch a runner off of a base. Each team kicks until they have made three outs, then the other team is up.

Play the game until dinner, but be sure to call in the runners who are still hiding in the woods, waiting for their opportunity to run to home base. Don't worry about rules—you can make them up as you go along. It's a wild game that you won't forget!

8:00-9:00 p.m. Campfire and Teaching #2

The format for this campfire is similar to Tuesday night. Allow the kids to share stories about their river-rafting expedition. You will probably not have to prime the pump this time. Look for similarities in the sharing to use as a segue into your teaching on God's promises. Ask questions like, "Did you have very little or very much control over your boat as an individual? How much did you have to depend on your guide to get you through the rapids?" Segue into your next teaching segment.

Teaching #2: Trusting God through believing in his promises

Ask, by a show of hands, how many young people have ever had someone they cared about abandon them unexpectedly. Have willing students share specifically about their experiences. Then read Matthew 28:18-20 to the group. Emphasize that Jesus promises to us never leave or forsake us, unlike parents, friends, or steady relationships who sometimes can and do.

Next, read Jeremiah 29:11. Point out that God has a plan for everyone, and it is a good one. His plan has a hope and a future, even though we may not always think so. Then ask, "Were there times when we were rafting today and you didn't think you'd make it? And times when you wondered if the boat guide knew what she was doing, yet she did? What parallels can we make from this Bible promise and our time today?" Allow time for responses.

Now, read Philippians 1:6. Paul says here that Jesus won't give up on us. Then say, "Was there anyone today or yesterday who believed in you when you didn't believe in yourself? God never gives up on us, even though we may think he has every right to do so."

Read 1 Corinthians 10:13. Point out that even though we may be tempted and think it is impossible to escape, God is faithful and always provides a way out. Ask, "Were there any times over the few days where it seemed that there was *no way* to accomplish the task of arriving at your destination, yet almost miraculously a way opened up that made it possible? What parallels can we find here for our lives?" Allow time for responses.

Next, read John 10:28-29. This Scripture teaches us that no one can snatch us out of the Father's hands, although at times it seems we may fall out. Ask, "Did you ever feel while rock climbing that you didn't want to trust the rope, particularly when climbing down a rock? How did that feel? What did you learn?" Allow time for responses.

9:00-10:00 p.m. Candle Passing

When you have finished Teaching #2, begin your candle passing ceremony. The goal is for each person to share one area they would like to trust God more with. Pass one lit candle around the group. As each person takes the candle, they share an area of their lives they want to more fully trust God with. No one talks except the person holding the candle. Anyone is allowed to pass if they wish. This exercise usually results in some great sharing. When a person holds a candle in a dark place, they feel less conscious of others. Kids also seem to take their answers more seriously when they can see their turn coming.

Close the evening with "popcorn prayer," directing the campers to pray one-sentence prayers in which they declare their trust in the Lord for specific areas of their lives. Such prayers could include sentences like, "I trust you, Jesus, for helping my father to get a job" or, " Lord, I trust you to help me over come my feelings of worthlessness." Allow this to continue until the prayers begin to diminish. Finish your time with a reflective song such as "Bind us Together."

7:30-8:00 a.m. Individual devotions

Have your campers read ten verses from Section Three of *The Personal Promise Pocketbook* entitled, "God's Promises and Purposes for my Relationships with Others". Tell everyone to pick one verse upon that they will meditate on throughout the day and on their way home.

EDITOR'S NOTE

Adventure retreats offer tremendous potential for your kids to grow and develop a stronger bond with each other and a high level of personal satisfaction. They also pose certain liabilities. Choose your outfitting organization carefully. I have worked with Craig and The Rock 'N Water gang and am very confident in their commitment to safety. When possible, a pre-visit is strongly encouraged, as well as obtaining a list of references from the organization that you can check with personally.

WALK A MILE IN MY SHOES

Kirk McCormick & Chris Cannon

THE BIG IDEA

Peer counselors are trained in basic helping skills such as empathy and active listening. They are also taught to develop and maintain a healthy attitude in peer ministry.

WHO SHOULD ATTEND

High school students who have been selected as peer counselors through an application process (see application form on page 116). This retreat works best with twenty or less peer counselors participating. This allows for the greatest amount of interaction and the greatest amount of training.

As you screen your peer counselor applicants, you should be looking for three basic qualities:
1. A growing commitment to Jesus Christ
2. A sense of God's call to be a caregiver
3. A willingness to undertake further training beyond this retreat weekend

LOCATION

Any cabin or retreat center that will accommodate your group.

TIME FRAME

Friday night to Sunday afternoon

WHAT TO BRING

✓ Sleeping bag
✓ Toiletries
✓ Bible
✓ Notebook
✓ Pen or pencil

NECESSARY INGREDIENTS

★ Active games such as *Pictionary, Trivial Pursuit,* and *Taboo*
★ Whiteboard and markers
★ Overhead projector and screen
★ Workbooks

(continued)

★ Communion elements
★ At least four short stories, such as *The Velveteen Rabbit* by Margory Williams, *The Iron Horse* by Bib Considyne, *Courage* by John Galsworthy, and *The Enchanted Bluff* by Willa Cather. All of these, and a wealth of other wonderful stories, are included in *The Book of Virtues*, edited by William Bennett and published by Simon & Schuster.
★ Prizes for the Listening Game
★ Meals (two breakfasts, two lunches, one dinner)
★ Snacks
★ Names for The Pretender Game
★ Pictures from magazines of people expressing a variety of emotions
★ Games for free time

SCHEDULE

FRIDAY

5:00 p.m.	Meet at church
5:30 p.m.	Leave for retreat center or cabin (dinner on the road)
7:00 p.m.	Arrive at cabin/retreat center, unpack and settle in
8:00 p.m.	The Pretender
8:30 p.m.	Training #1: Love Must be Sincere
10:30 p.m.	Snacks
11:00 p.m.	Games
12:30 a.m.	In bed
1:00 a.m.	Lights out

SATURDAY

7:30 a.m.	Wake up
8:00 a.m.	Breakfast
8:30 a.m.	Training #2: A Biblical Model for Caregiving
9:00 a.m.	Training #3: Issues Facing Teenagers
9:30 a.m.	Prayer time

SATURDAY

10:30 a.m.	Teaching #4: Pitfalls to Avoid in Caregiving
12:00 p.m.	Lunch
1:00 p.m.	Free time
5:30 p.m.	Dinner
7:00 p.m.	The Listening Game
11:30 p.m.	Lights out

SUNDAY

8:00 a.m.	Breakfast
8:45 a.m.	Quiet time
9:45 a.m.	Teaching #5: Components of Effective Caregiving
11:00 a.m.	Break/Snacks
11:15 a.m.	Role plays
12:00 p.m.	Communion
12:30 p.m.	Lunch
3:00 p.m.	Leave for church
5:00 p.m.	Final prayer and good-byes

RETREAT COMPONENTS

8:00-8:30 p.m. The Pretender

First, give each person a name of a famous real-life person or fictional character (e.g., Michael Jordan, Charlie Brown, Moses). When you say "Go," have the students ask each other yes or no questions to try and figure out one another's identities. Questions can include: "Are you living?" or "Were you in politics?" and so on. The person being asked the questions can give hints by making comments that the person they are pretending to be might make (e.g., for Moses: "I sure am tired of walking around *so* long"). Keep playing until everyone's names have been guessed. Bring enough names to play twice.

8:30-10:30 p.m. Training #1: Love Must be Sincere

Pass out magazine pictures you have previously clipped to each student so that everyone has one. These pictures should portray various displays of emotion— a mother grieving at a funeral, an athlete celebrating a victory, an elderly person in a thoughtful pose, etc. Ask each student to study the picture he or she is holding and answer the following questions:

> "What do you think is happening with the people in your picture?"
> (Accuracy is not as important as their ability to *imagine* what might be happening.)
> "How do you think the person or people in your picture are *feeling* at this moment?"

Allow a minute for each student to formulate some thoughts and then invite participation. Do not require everyone to share, but most everyone will want to talk about their pictures.

Next, read Romans 12:9. Point out that Webster's dictionary defines the word *sincere* as "honest; without hypocrisy, embellishment or exaggeration; earnest devotion without reservation." Then ask the students the following questions, allowing for informal sharing:

> "What does this definition mean to you?"
> "How can you tell if someone is being sincere or not?"
> "On a scale of one to ten, with ten being totally sincere, how sincere is your love for the other students in our youth group?"

Remind them that as peer counselors, they must model sincere love through their words and actions.

Now set up a role play that represents a typical youth group scenario in which a peer counselor might be involved. For instance, have one student act as if he or she is brand new to the youth group, and has come to see a peer counselor because he or she is lonely. Put the students in pairs and allow each person the opportunity to play both the role of peer helper and new visitor to the youth group.

After the role play pairs have finished, ask students to write down in their notebooks their answers to the following two questions:
"How does it *feel* when someone sincerely takes an interest in you?"
"How does it feel when someone *pretends* to take a sincere interest in you?"

After they've written their answers, have a few willing students share their answers aloud.

Now read John 11:1-44. Point out the example Jesus set for us of sincere love through this story. Then ask the following questions:
"Do you think Jesus knew Lazarus was dead, or that he was going to die (vss. 11-15)?"
"If he knew that Lazarus was dead, why was he moved so deeply (vss. 33, 35, and 38)?"
"What can we learn from this passage about sincere love?"

Close this session by breaking your students into pairs, and have them read 1 Corinthians 13:4-8 to each another. After both people have read it once, have them read it again, this time replacing the word *love* with their partner's first name. For instance, "Kirk is patient, Chris is kind," etc. This will result in some laughter, but instruct students to read through it again to each other. For instance, Chris reads to Kirk, "Kirk is patient, Kirk is kind, etc." After both have read the verses to each other, have them identify three areas of love they wish to see God help them to improve in. For example, Chris says he would like to be more patient, less jealous, and not provoked to anger. When each pair has finished, have them pray for each other. For instance, Kirk prays for the areas Chris shared, and vice versa.

11:00 p.m.-12:30 a.m. Games
The group will need some time to relax; they've already had a big teaching and it's only Friday night. Give them some time to play a few fun games like *Pictionary*, *Charades*, or *Trivial Pursuit*.

8:30-9:00 a.m. Teaching #2: A Biblical Model for Caregiving

Open by reading John 1:1-18. This passage verifies that Jesus is the Savior. Next read Hebrews 8; 9:11-15; and Romans 8:33-38. These passages identify Jesus as the High Priest. Point out that Jesus is the "Who" in pastoral care. We simply follow in the footsteps of our High Priest in caring for the flock as we train ourselves to care more effectively for others in our group. Next, note that the best pastoral care happens when we, as caregivers, remember three essential things:

1. We are not the Savior.
2. Jesus has been, is, and will continue to care for people long after we are gone.
3. We need to get the people we care for into the loving hands of Jesus.

Close in prayer. Encourage your students to pray short sentence prayers aloud, asking God to give them a clear understanding of their roles as caregivers. Allow five minutes for a short stretch and restroom break.

9:00-9:30 a.m. Teaching #3: Issues Facing Teenagers

Using the whiteboard, brainstorm a list of issues facing teenagers. Anything, no matter how big or small, should go on the board. Such a list could include sex, dating, peer pressure, school, parents, friends, divorce, homework, suicide, competition, drugs, alcohol, etc.

Next, break into groups of four with one adult leader per group. Using the list of issues, have your groups talk about how Jesus might view these issues. Would Jesus see some issues as more important than others? More threatening than others? Deserving of greater attention than others?

When your small groups have finished their discussions, bring everyone back together. Close this teaching time by making the following points:

1. The best caregiving happens when we see people and issues as Jesus sees them.
2. Jesus cares deeply for even what we would deem the "smallest" issues of our lives.
3. If we are to care as Jesus cares, we need to avoid the trap of value judgement.

9:30-10:30 a.m. Prayer time

Get the group back into their foursomes. Have each person in a foursome take five to ten minutes to share what is going on in his or her life. After each person shares, have the other three persons pray for him or her. Go around the small group until everyone has had a turn to share and have prayer.

Finish your prayer groups around 10:15 a.m.; then give everyone a fifteen-minute stretch, restroom, and snack break.

10:30 a.m.-12:00 p.m. Teaching #4: Pitfalls to Avoid in Caregiving
Use the following outline to make your group aware of the pitfalls in caregiving and how they can avoid them.

1. **The Simplicity Syndrome:** "Just pray" is not always the right answer. "If you only have faith" does not always work.

   Point: A simple approach is good. A simplistic answer is malpractice. Caregiving is not about having pat answers. Sometimes there are no answers.

   Discuss as a group: "How can we avoid being overly simplistic?" Possible answers might include:
   Take time to give a thoughtful response. Simplistic answers are often the result of a hurried listener.
   Instead of only giving one possible solution, ("Just pray . . ."), try to think creatively about several potential answers, giving the other person choices to consider.

2. **The Spastic Syndrome:** There are some people who can't wait to be counselors. They get all hyped about "helping" someone find the answers to his or her problems. Consider the axiom, "Fools jump in where angels fear to tread."

   Point: People who are too excited about solving the problems of the world can take on things they should avoid. Like a spastic muscle, they are more of a pain and nuisance than anything else.

   Discuss as a group: "How can we avoid jumping in where we should probably get help?" It is helpful to know what limits and boundaries to establish in peer ministry. Issues such as abuse, suicide, and eating disorders requires outside intervention and should not be tackled alone. Peer counselors need to know when and to whom to make referrals in such cases.

3. **The Self-Indulgence Syndrome:** "When I help someone, I get such a rush," says one student.

> Point: If we are motivated by anything other than the compassion of Christ, watch out. We may be caregiving for all the wrong reasons.

> Discuss as a group: "What is the proper motivation for being a caregiver?" Turn to Philippians 2:1-5 and see what our "attitude" should be in helping others. According to John 15:12-14, love is sacrificial, not self-indulgent. Effective peer helpers are willing to lay down their lives for their friends in obedience to Christ, not for their own glory or satisfaction.

4. **The Naive Syndrome:** Everything is not as it always appears. Sometimes people come to us with ulterior motives. Remember: There are always two sides to every story.

> Point: Always try to listen with a discerning ear. Try to avoid getting caught up in the emotions of a situation.

> Discuss as a group: "How can we avoid being naive listeners?" Proverbs 18:17 states, "The first to present his case seems right, till another comes forward to question him." How does this wisdom apply to peer counseling? List some situations that would require you to hear from both sides before any action or advice would be appropriate.

5. **The Flakiness Syndrome:** All too often a well-intentioned person says he or she will commit to helping someone, then subsequently flakes out. More damage happens when there is no follow up than if there was no contact at all.

> Point: Prayerfully consider the commitment it will take before you enter into a caregiving situation.

> Discuss as a group: "How much time does it take to give proper care?" Allow enough time for: 1) the problem to be solved; 2) response to the problem or issue; 3) prayer. If these three elements are not part of the helping process, proper care has not been given.

6. **The Wimp Syndrome:** Sometimes a caregiver must be confrontational. We must hold people accountable. Jesus forgave the woman caught in adultery, but left her with the challenge to "Go now and leave your life of sin" (John 8:11).

Point: The goal of caregiving is to bring someone back to wholeness. This can only occur when we are willing to lovingly tell the hard truth.

Discuss as a group: "When I have to confront someone with something I know they will not want to hear, I _____." (Have your students take turns completing the sentence) Possible answers might include:

> water it down.
> overcompensate by being aggressive or cold.
> get nervous and avoid the subject.

1:00-5:30 p.m. Free time

Provide several optional activities during this time. These will obviously be dependent upon your choice of a cabin or conference center. Several possibilities include:

- Hiking
- Miniature golf
- Basketball or volleyball
- Shopping
- Horseback riding

While it is not always possible, team building is facilitated by having everyone participate in the activities together. Therefore, it is suggested that these possibilities be "co-ed" friendly.

7:00-10:00 p.m. The Listening Game

The best caregivers are great listeners. Here is a game to help your students discover just how good of listeners they are.

Break your group into teams of four. Read one of the short stories you've brought with you to the whole group. When you've read the entire story, have one person from each group come forward. Provide chairs for each representative. When they're seated, ask a question about some element of the story you've just read. Whoever gets it right scores one hundred points for their team. For each question you ask, bring another person from each team to the front to compete.

This game can last a long time. Use at least four stories—you'll be amazed how much better the students hear the second, third, and fourth stories.

When you have finished your competition, close by saying, "Listening is one of the keys to good caregiving. It allows you to follow the story and keep the facts straight. Listening helps you to know what kind of follow up your counselee needs. Remember: Listening is the key to quality caregiving."

8:45-9:45 a.m. Quiet time

At breakfast, hand out quiet time question sheets to each student. When your students break up for their quiet times, have them read 2 Corinthians 5:14-21 and reflect on the questions found on their sheets:

> How does God use us in a "ministry of reconciliation?"
> What is a "ministry of reconciliation?"
> How can a caregiving ministry reconcile your friends to Christ?
> Which of your friends needs to be reconciled to Christ, or to another friend? (Pray for them.)
> Are *you* in need of reconciliation in some way? Offer it to the Lord.

9:45-11:00 a.m. Teaching #5: Components of Effective Caregiving

Open by pointing out that there are three essential ideas to keep in mind when caring for someone:

1. What is this person's need?
2. How can Jesus fulfill that need?
3. How can I get this person into the loving presence of the Father?

If you are trying to do more than this in pastoral caregiving, you are trying to do too much. When approached by a peer who seeks your help, the following seven steps will keep your caregiving in focus:

Pray immediately. Our example is Jesus who is continually before the Father interceding for us. You do not have to pray aloud with the person at the beginning of your conversation, but you need to offer the situation to God's purposes and plan. Prayer is your conduit to God's wisdom and insight.

Listen carefully. Keep in mind these keys to good listening:

> Alleviate distractions
> Look at the person
> Repeat what they say back to them occasionally
> Ask clarifying questions, when necessary
> Good listening is an art; practice it. If you have something you need to do, let the person know. Ask if you can get back together when you can be more attentive.

Define the need. Asking good questions will help you define the need. Ask *how* and *why* questions. One word answers don't count. Ask for further details and information. Be specific and personal with your questions. Don't be afraid, if your instincts lead, to ask probing questions that might help you better understand the issues at hand.

Evaluate the need. Ask yourself, "Is this something I can handle, or do I need to get help from my youth pastor or another adult? How might Jesus have been praying for this already? What relationship is broken? What would God say about how to reconcile the brokenness?"

Suggest a strategy. Remember that you're not in the self-help business. Christian caregivers seek to help a person get to God for his or her strength, hope and answers.

> Strategies you can suggest include: Asking God for forgiveness; praying for healing; encouraging the person to make it right with the person he or she is in conflict with; getting the person to the hospital (if the problem is medical); getting the person into treatment (if their problem is substance-related).

Release the person to the Father. You are not the person's savior. There are two ways we can release:
1. With the person, pray for them. Give them to God.
2. Away from the person, pray for them.

Follow up. Check in to see how their strategies are working out. You don't necessarily need to rehash the issue. You are simply letting the person know that you still care and are still praying for them.

11:15 a.m.-12:00 p.m. Role plays

Break your groups into pairs. One person in each pair plays the role of caregiver, the other plays the role of counselee. The counselee approaches the caregiver about a particular problem. Give each pair real-life issues to deal with such as a recent divorce, date rape, the breakup of a steady relationship, school stress, and parental conflict. When the first role play is completed, have each pair switch roles and give them a new role play scenario. You may wish to model this at the beginning by doing a role play with another adult leader, in front of the group.

12:00-12:30 p.m. Communion

To commemorate the reconciliation God has afforded you, celebrate the Lord's Supper together as a group in a manner appropriate to the theology and traditions of your church or organization.

AUTHORS' NOTE

This weekend is merely an introduction to peer counseling. It is *not* a complete training experience. To properly train your caregivers, we recommend you use *Peer Counseling in Youth Groups* and *Advanced Peer Counseling in Youth Groups* by Joan Sturkie and Siang-Yang Tan (Youth Specialties). They can be ordered by calling toll-free 1-800-776-8008.

PEER COUNSELING APPLICATION

Name _____ Date _____

1. Why would you like to be a peer counselor?

2. Relate one experience you have had that shaped your desire to be in peer ministry.

3. What fears do you have about being in peer counseling?

4. Are you a good listener? Relate one example in your life in which you displayed good listening skills.

5. What problems do you think many of your peers struggle with that you might be required to help?

6. Peer ministry requires you to be assertive, sometimes telling people things they don't wan to hear. How do you feel about that?

7. What other commitments do you have this year that are extracurricular? [Note: You will be required to attend a weekend training retreat and mandatory weekly training meetings.]

UNDERSTANDING EACH OTHER

Kirk McCormick

THE BIG IDEAS

This retreat is designed to bring parents and kids together to explore a Christlike model for family relationships, improve family relationships, develop stronger relational skills, and strengthen families with a fun and memorable weekend.

WHO SHOULD ATTEND

All families are encouraged to attend, but it is required that both parents or stepparents attend, not just one or the other (unless, of course, there's only one parent in the home). This retreat works best with at least six families and no more than twelve.

LOCATION

A retreat center that can accommodate your whole group.

TIME FRAME

Friday evening to Sunday noon

WHAT TO BRING

✓ Sleeping bag
✓ Toiletries
✓ Flashlight
✓ Bible
✓ Notebook
✓ Pen or pencil

NECESSARY INGREDIENTS

★ VCR and TV monitor
★ The movie *Hook* (available at most video stores)
★ Overhead projector and screen
★ Transparency of *A Model for Parent/Teen Relationships* (page 128)
★ Whiteboard, markers and erasers
★ Two air horns (like the small emergency ones for boats, available at most sporting goods stores)
★ *What's Your Opinion?* questionnaires (page 127)
★ Extra Bibles
★ Blindfolds

(continued)

NECESSARY INGREDIENTS

★ Snacks
★ Short story for the *Listening Game* (Possible short stories include *The Velveteen Rabbit* by Margory Williams, *The Iron Horse* by Bib Considyne, *Courage* by John Galsworthy, and *The Enchanted Bluff* by Willa Cather. All of these, and a wealth of other wonderful stories, are included in *The Book of Virtues*, edited by William Bennett and published by Simon & Schuster.
★ Meals (Friday night B.B.Q. dinner at the church, one additional dinner, two lunches, and two breakfasts)

SCHEDULE

FRIDAY

6:30 p.m.	Meet at church for B.B.Q. dinner
7:30 p.m.	Opening discussion
8:30 p.m.	Leave for cabin/retreat center
10:30 p.m.	Arrive at cabin/retreat center
11:30 p.m.	Lights out

SATURDAY

1:00 p.m.	Free time
5:30 p.m.	Dinner
6:30 p.m.	Evening program: Family Feud
8:00 p.m.	Video: *Hook*
10:15 p.m.	Free time
11:00 p.m.	Bed time

SATURDAY

7:00 a.m.	Breakfast
7:30 a.m.	Morning Walk
9:00 a.m.	Morning meeting #1: Understanding God's Plan for Parent/Teen Relationships
11:10 a.m.	Break time
11:30 a.m.	Parent/teen discussion
12:30 p.m.	Lunch

SUNDAY

8:00 a.m.	Breakfast
8:30 a.m.	Blind Walk
9:00 a.m.	Debrief
9:15 a.m.	Morning meeting #2: Biblical Principles for Good Communication
10:00 a.m.	Bathroom break
10:15 a.m.	The Listening Game
10:40 a.m.	Communication exercise
11:30 a.m.	Debrief
12:00 p.m.	Lunch

RETREAT COMPONENTS

6:30-7:30 p.m. Meet at church for B.B.Q. dinner

At the dinner (hamburgers, salad, chips, and sodas), pass out copies of the questionnaire *What's Your Opinion?* (see page 127). It is vitally important that everyone fills out a questionnaire. Collect the questionnaires and take them with you to the retreat center.

7:30-8:30 p.m. Opening discussion

Have your students and parents break into groups of no more than seven persons each, students with students and parents with parents. Have the groups discuss the following questions:
1. Why did you come on this retreat?
2. What would you like to have happen during your time on this retreat?
3. What is the one thing you least understand about your parent/teenager?

Provide a maximum of twenty minutes for these questions. Then have each group pick one spokesperson. Have each spokesperson share the group's responses to the questions. Write on on your whiteboard each group's responses to questions two and three.

Next, make these points to the group:

> "Two major reasons why most teens and parents have problems in their relationships are *a lack of understanding* and *poor communication skills.*"

> "Our hope for this retreat is to give you all a better understanding of one another, and to provide you with some simple communication tools to enrich your relationships."

Close with prayer for the weekend and your travel. Excuse people to their cars or the church vehicle(s) and depart for the retreat center.

10:30-11:30 p.m. Arrive at the cabin/retreat center

Assign cabins. Go to cabins. Encourage families to pray together for the weekend before they retire.

7:30-8:30 a.m. Morning Walk

After breakfast, bring everyone back together. Bring out the *What's Your Opinion?* questionnaires from the night before and read some of the responses to the group. Ask willing kids and adults to share some of their answers to the questions.

When you've finished reviewing the questionnaires, send parents and teens, in their family units, on a morning walk. During their walks, their assignments are to listen to each other's responses. The one ground rule is that no one is allowed to criticize anyone else's responses. Remind them to meet back at the meeting room at 9:00 a.m. sharp, with their Bibles and pens/pencils.

9:00-11:10 a.m.
Morning meeting #1: Understanding God's Plan for Parent/Teen Relationships
Scripture: Ephesians 6:1-4

Begin with everyone in a large group. Tell this story (or one from your experience with a similar punch line):

> "There was once a man who decided to build a house. So he went around to different neighborhoods looking at various houses, choosing qualities about those houses that he liked. When he had decided to start his dream home, he completed a set of plans from which he would build his home. The problem was, he had no idea *how* to build a home, even though he had seen plenty of beautifully built homes. Nevertheless, he started building his home. Upon completion, the man saw that his floor was cracked, his walls leaned, his roof leaked, his windows seeped, his doors jammed, and his electrical system was faulty. It was then—and only then—that the man considered that perhaps he should have consulted a contractor."

When you've finished your story, say, "Most of us have seen some pretty good parent/teen relationships. But very few of us would consider ourselves experts when it comes to being a parent or teenager. In fact, if there are any perfect parents in this room, please stand." (Nobody stands, of course.) "Now, if there are any perfect teenagers in this room, please stand." (Again, nobody stands.) "Truth is, we all usually learn the hard way, by trial and error.

"What if we were able to admit that we need the help of a master builder as we construct our relationships with our parents or teens? As Christians, we have the privilege of consulting *the* expert on parent/teen relationships, our heavenly Father. This morning, we want to look at God's master plan for parent/child relationships."

Next, have everyone turn to Ephesians 6:1-4. Read the Scripture aloud, then make the following brief points (no longer than one minute for each point):

> "This passage captures the Bible's teaching on parent/child relationships. God's plan is summarized right here."

> "Things start to go wrong when children stop honoring their parent(s), or when parents start exasperating their children. *Both cases are equally wrong according to God's plan.*"

Now, have the group break into all-parent and all-teen discussion groups again, preferably different ones from last night. Have each group pick a spokesperson. Ask each group to answer the following questions:
>Why do teenagers sometimes dishonor their parents?
>Why do parents sometimes exasperate their teens?
>What do parents *not* understand about teens?
>What do teens *not* understand about parents?

Give out the questions one at a time. After each question has been discussed by the groups, have the spokespersons for each group share their group's answers.

When you've finished the questions, bring everyone back together as a large group. Ask the group to come up with synonyms for "honor." Next, have them come up with synonyms for "exasperate." Write their suggestions on the white-board.

[NOTE: Before you get into the next section, take a ten to fifteen minute bathroom break.]

When you've re-formed your group, place a transparency of *A Model for Parent/Teen Relationships* (found on page 128) on your overhead projector. Wrap up the morning session by exploring God's plan for parent/teen relationships and what happens when the plan goes awry.

Understanding the Model
1. Each axis represents the attitude or motivation of a parent (the horizontal axis) or teen (the vertical axis) as he/she is in relation with his/her parent or teen. Parents tend to float between relating out of Authority (God's plan), and Power (the corrupted plan). Teenagers tend to float between relating out of Respect (God's plan) and Defiance (the corrupted plan). Authority and Respect are motivated by love, and are positive building blocks. "Power" and "Defiance" are motivated by pride, ego, fear, and/or selfishness, and are destructive to parent/teen relationships.

2. God's plan comes together in the upper right quadrant of the model. The parent exercises authority and the teen exercises respect. The parent lets his or her wishes be known, and the teen, whether he or she agrees or not, responds to the wish. Much compromise and discussion happens in this quadrant.

   Sometimes a parent *demands* respect from a teen. This is a Power play. Although the teen may respond with Respect, the situation is not as positive as it can be because the parent has "exasperated" the teen. Likewise, sometimes the teen rebels against the parent, even though the parent comes to the teen in the God-given position of Authority. The worst case is when the parent is in Power and the teen is in Defiance. This is a lose-lose situation.

3. This is, of course, a simplistic model for parent/teen relations. But this model does demonstrate that, when both parent and teen build their relationship out of mutual love for God and each other, wholeness occurs.

Summarize your teaching with the following observations:

Healthy parent/teen relationships are the result of healthy individual contributions. Both parents and teens need to bring an intentional, positive, godly, love-motivated attitude to their relationships if both want the best relationship possible.

Relating through Power (for the parent) or Defiance (for the teen) will create distress, if not a rupture, in parent/teen relationships.

You can only change YOU. No measure of manipulation or control can transform your parent/teen.

We are all accountable to God, first and foremost. It is through striving to live out our family relationships, according to God's plan, that we learn to be the best parent/teen possible. God is the heavenly Father as well as the only begotten Son. God understands the life of the parent and the teenager.

Close with prayer. Encourage willing parents and teens to speak out with one-sentence prayers, asking God to help them build healthier relationships with their parent/teen.

11:30 a.m.-12:30 p.m. Parent/teen discussion
Break your group into their respective family units. Have them break off and discuss the following questions, encouraging them to be as open, honest, and loving as they can:

1. Where do you see your relationships falling in the Authority/Power and Respect/Defiance grid?

2. How do each of you feel when your parents operate out of the Authority mode? Conversely, how do each of you feel when your parents operate out of the Power mode? (Share specific examples.)

3. How do each of you feel when your teens operate out of the Respect mode? Conversely, how do each of you feel when your teens operate out of the Defiance mode? (Again, be specific.)

4. How can the teens better demonstrate respect?

5. How can the parents better exercise authority?

1:00-5:30 p.m. Free time

This time should be divided into two sections. During the first two hours, provide options for families to spend time together to facilitate communication. Some ideas include:

- Hiking
- Walking
- Bicycle riding

Some families may wish to join together during this time. While this is acceptable, the teens will tend to congregate with other teens, and eliminate the desired outcome of families building a memory.

From 3:00-5:00 p.m., provide structured recreational activities or games for the youth. (By this time, they will probably be dying to get away from their parents, and vice versa!) Some ideas include:

- Volleyball
- Ropes course (if available)
- Capture the Flag
- Steal the Bacon
- Rock climbing

Before you embark on this retreat, research the surrounding areas near your retreat site for possible recreational activities for families and kids. Give families a list of possibilities after lunch Saturday. They will appreciate your thoughtfulness.

6:30-8:00 p.m. Evening program: Family Feud

Break the group into two teams, parents and teens. Using the *What's Your Opinion?* questionnaire, go down the list of questions. For each question, the subject group (for example, parents) must agree on one group answer. Then the other team (in this case, teams) must try to guess the answer. Award one thousand points for correct answers. Have fun with this, encouraging a lot of yelling, gesturing, and laughter. At the end of the game, point out how the questions demonstrate that teens and parents have different ideas about what the other is thinking. Give yourself about an hour to play the game.

Now, bring your group back together for a large-group discussion. Lead an informal discussion, centering on the theme, "Understanding Each Other." Using the questions and answers from the Family Feud, try to get the teens and parents to better understand why they act and think differently. Say something like, "How many of you parents were surprised when the number one answer from the teens about what bugs them about parents was . . . ? Why were you surprised?" "Why do you teenagers think your parents are so conservative about when you can start dating?"

Keep the discussion going for as long as it seems people are into it (or until 7:45 p.m., whichever comes first), then take a break.

8:00-10:15 p.m. Video: *Hook*

Show the movie *Hook*. Have snacks available. Encourage the group to watch the movie in light of all that they have discussed so far. Tell them to be ready to critique the film's characters afterwards.

After you've shown the movie, talk about how Robin Williams changed as a parent. How did his kids react to him in the beginning of the film as opposed to the end? How did their relationship change? Why?

[**Note:** Preview the movie prior to the retreat so you will be ready to lead an effective discussion. Also, make sure you're satisfied that the language and situations in this video are appropriate for your group. If not, substitute another video or activity.]

8:30-9:00 a.m. Blind Walk

Give each family unit several blindfolds. Each family unit must lead the blindfolded members of their family on two 15-minute walks. First, have parents lead their blindfolded teens. At the fifteen-minute mark, have the kids lead their blindfolded parents. The point of this exercise is to encourage trust and communication among family members.

9:00-9:15 a.m. Debrief

Bring everyone together and have the families share their experiences. How hard was it to listen and take directions? What were some of the obstacles in communication? Was it easy to trust one another? Why or why not? The point of the debriefing is to begin a discussion on effective parent/teen communication, the other goal of the weekend.

9:15-10:00 a.m. Morning meeting #2: Biblical Principles for Good Communication

Select volunteers to read the following verses aloud, one passage at a time:
> Colossians 3:9-10 (honesty)
> Galatians 5:22-23 (patience)
> 1 Peter 2:17 (respect)
> Proverbs 1:5 (listening)
> Colossians 3:16-17 (godly attitude)

After each passage is read, lead a discussion using the following questions:
> "What can this passage teach us about better communicating with and understanding each other?"
> "What disrupts our ability to do what these verses encourage us to do?"

You can have a lot of fun with this. Get people to give examples, both positive and negative, of what these look like and how they effect relationships. The key is to demonstrate that good communication does not just happen; it is the by-product of hard work.

10:15-10:40 a.m. The Listening Game

Divide the group into two mixed teams, with teens and adults on each team. Read aloud the short story you have selected. After you have read the story once, ask questions about the story, which both teams try to be the first to correctly answer. The team that gets the most answers right, wins. This is a good game to demonstrate how well people listen.

10:40-11:30 a.m. Communication exercise

Break the group back into their respective family units. Then break the family units into pairs (or threes if necessary). Have your teens and parents respond to one another, using the following statements. When a parent or teen has completed a sentence, the listener(s) repeats what the responder said, only using different words. As time allows, allow families to delve deeper into issues raised by these statements:

(Teen)	"Sometimes I don't think you understand that I . . . "
(Parent)	"Sometimes I don't think that you understand that I . . . "
(Parent)	"I get frustrated in our relationship when . . . "
(Teen)	"I get frustrated in our relationship when . . . "
(Teen)	"The hardest part of living my life is . . . "
(Parent)	"The hardest part of living my life is . . . "
(Parent)	"The characteristic I like the most about you is . . . "
(Teen)	"The characteristic I like the most about you is . . . "
(Teen)	"The thing I would like to work on with you is . . . "
(Parent)	"The thing I would like to work on with you is . . . "

11:30 a.m.-12:00 p.m. Debrief

Finally, lead the group in a debrief about the weekend. What did they learn about themselves, their parent(s) or child(ren)? How can their relationships grow? What are they committing to work on? What was the highlight of the weekend? What was the lowlight of the weekend? Add your own questions as you see fit.

Reread Ephesians 6:1-4 as a benediction; then form a circle and close your weekend with a time of prayer.

WHAT'S YOUR OPINION?

We'd like to know your opinion on the following statements and questions.

I am a: parent   teenager   (circle one)

The three most commonly used phrases by a parent are:

The three most commonly used phases by a teenager are:

Parents do not understand teenagers in the following three areas:

Teenagers do not understand parents in the following three areas:

How many nights during the school week should teenagers be allowed to go out?

What should a teenager's curfew be on a school night?

At what age should a teenager be allowed to start dating?

At what age should a teenager have their driver's license?

The top three things that bug teenagers about their parents are:

The top three things that bug parents about their teenagers are:

The hardest thing about being a teenager is:

The hardest thing about being a parent is:

A MODEL FOR PARENT/TEEN RELATIONSHIPS

Thesis: Parents and their teenagers float along their respective axes as they relate to one another. The result is, in general terms, one of four outcomes (one of which is ideally positive).

Horizontal Axis: Parent
Vertical Axis: Teenager

(+) Respect

Motivation: Parent - Love
Teen - Love

Outcome: Ideally Positive, Fulfilling

Motivation: Parent - Pride, Ego, Frustration, etc.
Teen - Love

Outcome: Parent - False Gratification
Teen - Disappointed Submission

(+) Authority ———————————————————— **(-) Power**

Motivation: Parent - Love
Teen - Pride, Ego, Frustration, etc.

Outcome: Parent - Empty sense of satisfaction
Teen - Reluctant Obedience

Motivation: Parent - Pride, Ego, Frustration, etc.
Teen - Pride, Ego, Frustration, etc.

Outcome: Chaos, Rebellion, Anger, Selfishness, Painfully Negative

(-) Defiance

"Authority" -   The benevolent guidance of a loving leader. Something exercised, not demanded.
"Power" -   The unilateral control over someone regardless of that person's wishes. Something seized, not received.
"Respect" -   The willingness to be subject to someone else. Something given not demanded.
"Defiance" -   The arrogant, self-serving lack of regard for someone else's feelings and wishes. Something seized, not received.

LAND OF THE GIANTS

Steve Moyer

THE BIG IDEA

A camping retreat designed to prepare incoming ninth graders for the challenges and opportunities that high school will present them, and provide them with tools to meet those challenges and opportunities.

WHO SHOULD ATTEND

All incoming ninth graders.

LOCATION

Any campsite that can accommodate your size group.

TIME FRAME

Friday night to Sunday afternoon

WHAT TO BRING

✓ Camping gear
✓ Hiking boots
✓ Sleeping bags
✓ Air mattresses
✓ Toiletries
✓ Bible
✓ Notebook
✓ Pen or pencil
✓ Flashlight
✓ Sunscreen
✓ Insect repellent

NECESSARY INGREDIENTS

★ Tents
★ Propane or liquid fuel camp stoves and lanterns
★ Cooking utensils (pots, pans, spatulas, ladles, can and bottle openers, cutlery)
★ Portable charcoal or propane grill
★ Ice chests
★ Dishwashing supplies (soap, tubs, towels, etc.)
★ Meals (two breakfasts, two lunches, one dinner)
★ High-powered flashlight for Escaped Convict
★ Snacks

(continued)

NECESSARY INGREDIENTS

★ Marshmallows, graham crackers, and chocolate bars for S'Mores
★ Any other camping equipment that you may feel is necessary
★ Old high school yearbooks from adult volunteers
★ Video camera and blank videocassette

TRANSPORTATION

Depending on the gear you bring, you may need full-size cars to carry students and gear, or you might get one truck or van for all the equipment and cars for the students. Since camping gear can take up a great deal of space, I prefer the truck method.

SCHEDULE

FRIDAY

[**Note:** All participants to eat dinner before arriving at church]

6:00 p.m.	Meet at church/leave for campsite
7:30 p.m.	Arrive at campsite/set up
9:30 p.m.	Campfire
10:30 p.m.	Escaped Convict
12:00 a.m.	Lights out

SATURDAY

6:00 p.m.	Dinner
7:00 p.m.	Teaching #1: Seeing the Possibilities
8:30 p.m.	Campfire
10:30 p.m.	Escaped Convict
11:30 p.m.	Sardines
12:30 a.m.	Lights out

SATURDAY

7:00 a.m.	Wake up
7:30 a.m.	Breakfast
8:15 a.m.	Quiet time
9:00 a.m.	Structured activities
12:00 p.m.	Lunch
1:00 p.m.	Free time/recreation (collect five rocks)
5:00 p.m.	Reassemble and review the day

SUNDAY

7:00 a.m.	Wake up
7:30 a.m.	Breakfast
8:30 a.m.	Quiet time
9:00 a.m.	Teaching #2: David and Goliath
11:00 a.m.	Break camp
12:00 p.m.	Lunch
12:30 p.m.	Testimonies
1:15 p.m.	Leave for home

RETREAT COMPONENTS

FRIDAY

6:00 p.m. Meet at church/leave for campsite

Leave early enough to get to the campsite *before* dusk. It is extremely difficult to set up camp in the dark. Familiarize yourself with how to set up your tents before you leave, so this process will be easier.

9:30 p.m. Campfire

To help break the ice, have your adult leaders share humorous stories about when they were incoming ninth graders. For a good laugh, have them pass their high school yearbooks around the campfire as they tell their stories. Follow the stories with one of your own, then lead a fun singing time. When you're done singing, S'mores are a must.

10:30 p.m. Escaped Convict

Find an area about forty yards long that has lots of trees and bushes. The goal is for students to get from one end of the area to the other without getting caught.

Take a high-powered flashlight and back up about twenty yards from the game area. Turn on the flashlight and slowly sweep the beam from one end to the other and back again. If any students are caught in the beam, they are out of the round. They will hide behind bushes and trees as the light sweeps by. You must always sweep froward with the beam until it reaches the designated end point, and only then can you go backward until your beam reaches the starting point. The students will then figure out that they are to run as the beam passes them. You can speed up the beam on occasion, but you cannot cross kids up by suddenly switching direction or pattern. Play several rounds, from both ends of your play area. If possible, set up in a new area after a few rounds.

8:15 a.m. Quiet time

Have your students read and reflect on Psalm 37 and Numbers 13 about the spies in the land. Let students wander off to read it by themselves, pray, and generally be silent. Students get very reflective when camping. Encourage them to journal if they wish.

9:00 a.m. Structured activities

Offer a variety of activities to appeal to different interests. Options can include an all-day or half-day hike, inner tubing or swimming if you are near a river, and rock climbing if you have the opportunity, equipment, and training. Offer three or so activities, and have students select one of them. One goal for this time is to get your campers to see things from a new perspective, whether it is looking off the mountain, down from a rock, or toward shore from the water. These make great object lessons for the teaching in the evening.

1:00 p.m. Free time/recreation

You can keep this time totally unstructured, or offer some games such as Capture the Flag, Scavenger Hunt, Frisbee Golf, etc. Be on the lookout for students who seem left out. This can be a good opportunity for you and your adult leaders to spend one-on-one time with certain students.

Give your kids one assignment to complete during free time: each student is to collect five rocks to bring to the evening session.

5:00 p.m. Reassemble and review the day

This can be fairly unstructured, but it is an important time to reconnect with your students. There will be many stories to tell about the hikes and games! You can also remind your kids to collect their five rocks for tonight's session.

7:00 p.m. Teaching #1: Seeing the Possibilities (Numbers 13)

The goal of this teaching is to help your incoming ninth graders to see the potential, not the problems, of their upcoming high school years. Read Numbers 13 aloud in a circle, having everyone take turns reading one verse at a time. Then ask the following questions:

"What did Caleb and Joshua see that excited them?"
"What did the other men see?"
"How do you explain the difference in perspective?

"What can you learn from this story as it relates to your involvement in the high school group?"

"Are there any 'giants' in your life that are keeping you from having something special?"

Immediately after the last question, break the students into groups of two to four, with at least one older high school student or adult in every group. Repeat the questions one at a time, and have them discuss their answers in these small groups, followed by a short time of prayer together.

Following this time, have one of your high school juniors or seniors present do a teaching on the five smooth stones that David brought to defeat the giant. A typical teaching might sound something like this:

"The five 'stones' that helped me as a ninth grader to overcome my fears and insecurities were:
1. Regular youth group attendance
2. Praying on a regular basis
3. Getting to know one of the adult staff pretty well and being discipled by him/her
4. Getting involved in a campus Bible study
5. Going on as many youth group activities as I possibly could."

Each student should have five stones or rocks they collected during free time. Have each kid identify five things they would like to do to make their high school years some of their best ever in the Christian walk. Encourage them to take their stones home as a reminder of their goals. Close this time with a battle song or a song of declaration such as "Our God Reigns," "Our God is an Awesome God," or "Shine, Jesus, Shine."

8:30 p.m. Campfire

Songs and S'Mores are a must, of course. This is also an opportunity for a directed question-and-answer time. Encourage kids to ask any questions that are on their minds—about their faith, ninth grade, their hopes, fears, etc. Songs can be sung in between sharing. Prayers can also be offered. Don't worry about whether the students will share or not, they will. And long periods of silence are great when you're around a campfire.

10:30 p.m. Escaped Convict

Trust me, they will want to play it again!

11:30 p.m. Sardines

Send two people off to hide within a designated area. After four minutes, everyone else goes and looks for them. If you find them, hide with them in the same spot. By the time the last person finds the group, they will look like sardines all scrunched up behind a bush. The first person/pair who found them hides next.

SUNDAY

8:30 a.m. Quiet time

Have the students read and reflect on 1 Samuel 17:1-51, the story of David and Goliath. Challenge them to spend significant time in prayer—at least ten minutes (which is a long time for a young teen).

9:00 a.m. Teaching #2: David and Goliath

This is a similar format as the evening before, except that you do not need to read the text, since they have just read it during their quiet time. Once the students have reassembled, ask the following questions:

"Why was David confident he could defeat Goliath?"

"What do you think was different about David as compared to the Israelites who wouldn't fight Goliath?"

"What are some examples in your life where you have seen God's strength demonstrated?"

"How has that helped you to be 'more than a conqueror' in other areas of your life?"

You can choose to stay in the large group and have the kids raise their hands to answer questions. Feel free to add your own follow-up questions when you feel it will be helpful to that person and/or the whole group. Otherwise, have the campers answer in small groups, as you did the night before.

Close your time with a prayer circle. Place all your ninth graders in the middle of your circle, and have the adult leaders lay hands on the ninth graders as you lead a prayer of commissioning for them.

12:30 p.m. Testimonies

Before you leave, invite brief testimonies from the ninth graders. Encourage them to share what they have learned about conquering the giants in the land (you may wish to videotape this and show it at your senior banquet in four years!). End this time when the sharing begins to wane (they may have already made their declarations during the earlier session), and form a circle for a group hug.

September Kickoff

Ed Kelley

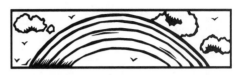

THE BIG IDEA
This retreat is designed to help students understand your philosophy of worship and begin their school year with the habit of quiet times and devotions.

WHO SHOULD ATTEND
All interested high school students who are serious about deepening their walk with Jesus.

LOCATION
A hotel, resort, or retreat center that can accommodate your entire group.

TIME FRAME
Friday afternoon to Sunday afternoon

WHAT TO BRING
- ✓ Sleeping bag
- ✓ Pillow
- ✓ Toiletries
- ✓ Bible
- ✓ Pen or pencil

NECESSARY INGREDIENTS
- ★ Meals (two dinners, two lunches, two breakfasts)
- ★ Snacks
- ★ Bread and grape juice for communion
- ★ Worship leader or team
- ★ Whiteboard or easel with markers
- ★ Song sheets with lyrics to the songs or overheads with projector
- ★ 3-by-5 cards
- ★ Pens/papers or a retreat booklet
- ★ Metal trash can
- ★ Matches
- ★ Board games like *Trivial Pursuit*, *Monopoly*, and *Risk*

SCHEDULE

FRIDAY

4:00 p.m.	Meet at church for registration
5:30 p.m.	Arrive at cabin or retreat center
6:15 p.m.	Pizza and activity
9:00 p.m.	Worship
9:45 p.m.	Break
10:00 p.m.	Session #1: Real Worship I
11:00 p.m.	Small groups
12:00 a.m.	Lights out

SUNDAY

7:30 a.m.	Wake up
8:00 a.m.	Optional seminar: Who am I in Christ?
8:30 a.m.	Breakfast
9:15 a.m.	Quiet time
10:00 a.m.	Worship and communion
10:45 a.m.	Break to change
11:00 a.m.	Italian Softball
12:00 p.m.	Lunch
12:45 p.m.	Pack it up
1:30 p.m.	Group photo and circle of prayer
2:00 p.m.	Leave for home
4:00 p.m.	Arrive back at church

SATURDAY

7:00 a.m.	Wake up
7:30 a.m.	Optional seminar: Jesus Qualities
8:00 a.m.	Breakfast
8:45 a.m.	Worship
9:00 a.m.	Quiet time
9:45 a.m.	Session #2: Real Worship II
11:00 a.m.	Break
11:20 a.m.	Four-Way Volleyball
12:00 p.m.	Lunch
12:45 p.m.	Announcements
1:00 p.m.	Recreation time
5:30 p.m.	Clean up for dinner
6:00 p.m.	Dinner
7:00 p.m.	Session #3: Real Worship III
9:00 p.m.	Break/Snack
9:20 p.m.	Sharing
10:00 p.m.	Free time
11:00 p.m.	Small groups
11:45 p.m.	Lights out

RETREAT COMPONENTS

FRIDAY

6:15-9:00 p.m. Pizza and activity

Be sure to have the number of a local pizza place that delivers before you arrive at the cabin. Then you can call for pizza right away when you arrive, unless you choose to take the group out for pizza on the way to your activity.

Activities can include miniature golf, bowling, or other fun activities that are available within a reasonable distance from your site. (Build the cost of these events into the price of your retreat.)

9:00-9:45 p.m. Worship

Begin the session with fast songs like "Thanks be to God" and "King Jesus is All." After a few songs, have a student share a five-minute testimony about what the Lord is doing in his or her life. (Arrange this ahead of time with a willing student.)

Next, move into slower worship songs like "Oh Lord, You're Beautiful" and "Trust in the Lord." When you've finished singing, give the students an orientation of the weekend's events. Then, ask them to share their goals for the weekend. Let this time be an open forum so that all of the kids who want to share get a chance. Goals can include, "I want to get to know God better this weekend," or "I'm here to learn more about worship."

10:00-11:00 p.m. Session #1: Real Worship I

Begin this session with a few faster songs like "Jesus is my Rock" and "River of Life," then focusing on slower songs like "I Love you Lord" and "I Will be Still."

Then, introduce your session with the following question: "When we think of God, what do we think of?"

Have the students share their answers freely, and write all their responses down on a whiteboard. When you've written down their answers, point out that preconceived ideas without facts and/or experience are dangerous. The key to healthy worship lies in our view of God.

Next, have your group look up Proverbs 9:10. This verse tells us that without knowledge of God, all worship is unacceptable worship, not any different than idolatry. We think of idolatry as a pagan in a hut with a little statue; actually it's thinking any thoughts about God that are untrue of him or that are unworthy of him.

Now, have your group look up Psalm 50:21. While our culture has brought God down to our level as a buddy or a pal, he is *holy, awesome,* and *majestic*. Read the following quote from A.W. Tozer:

> "The history of mankind will probably show that no people has ever risen above its religion, and man's spiritual history will positively demonstrate that no religion has ever been greater than its idea of God. . . . For this reason the gravest question before the church is always God Himself, and the most portentous fact about any man is not what he at a given time may say or do, but what he in his deep heart conceives God to be like."
> (*The Knowledge of the Holy*, 1961, Harper Brothers).

Ask your group, "So who is God?"

God is unchanging (read James 1:7 and Psalms 102:25-26). Change is usually for better or for worse. God doesn't change because he doesn't get any better and he wouldn't get any worse. When we talk of God not changing, we mean his will or character. The stuff he is inside!

Then ask, "What does this mean to you, the Christian?"
1. God's love is forever—no matter where you've been in your life.

2. His forgiveness is forever—no matter what you've done.

3. His security is forever—not like a hotel reservation that gets lost or an airline flight that's canceled. Once you're *truly* in, he doesn't let go!

Now ask, "What does that mean to you, the seeker?"
1. Your soul will die if sin is present and you've failed to repent. It will happen. God won't change his mind and let you in the back door.

2. Though saddened, he will not force those who have snubbed him to enter into his kingdom.

Close with, "The bottom line is this: It's important how you view God—what you think of him, and how accurate that is to what he's really like."

Next, give everyone a 3-by-5 card. Tell them to write out all that they know about God in a few paragraphs. They can use as much of the card as they wish. Encourage them to be honest. Tell them you don't want their names on the cards, just their thoughts.

Collect all of the cards and use them to correct and reinforce your kids' views of God during the upcoming year. (You'll find this exercise quite eye-opening.)

Close with prayer and a final worship song. Then tell them that tomorrow, you'll look at another quality of God. Encourage students to "meet" God this weekend, to be open to the Spirit revealing things about themselves and their Master. Dismiss the students to their rooms for small group discussion and lights out.

11:00 p.m.-12:00 a.m. Small groups
Let the students take a short break and say goodnight to their friends, then get them to their rooms for small group time.

During the small group time, encourage your room leaders to discuss any questions that the kids may have from the evening session. Have your room leaders ask kids to then discuss what they think it means to "know God." Have the small groups close in prayer before lights out.

SATURDAY

7:30-8:00 a.m. Optional seminar: Jesus Qualities
This is for students who are early risers and are motivated to learn more. Hold this seminar away from traffic flow, to discourage latecomers and reduce distractions.

Ask the students how the following statements about Jesus can strengthen and encourage them:

John 11:25	(He is the Resurrection)
John 14:6	(He is the Way, the Truth and the Life)
John 8:12	(He is the Light of the World)
Isaiah 9:6	(He is Wonderful)
Isaiah 9:6	(He is Counselor)
Isaiah 9:6	(He is the Prince of Peace)
Isaiah 7:14	(He is Immanuel)

After the students have shared, tell each one to select one of these Jesus qualities to focus on as he or she worships him today.

8:45-9:00 a.m. Worship
Start with two fast worship songs like "Pharaoh, Pharaoh" and "Heaven's Inn." Then move on to slower praise songs. Five slow songs are suggested, such as, "Strength of my Life," "Humble Thyself," "Majesty," "As the Deer," and "I Will be Still."

9:00-9:45 a.m. Quiet time
Give the students instructions on quiet time. Let them know if you want them to go outside and find a quiet spot, go back to their cabins, or stay where they are. There is to be no talking during quiet time.

For their quiet time, tell them to read Psalm 134 and Psalm 40:1-5, then rewrite these passages in their own words.

9:45-11:00 a.m. Session #2: Real Worship II
Start with three or four fast songs. It's fine to use songs you've already sung. Next, have two or three willing students share testimonies from the activities of the previous night. Have them share about anything that touched them during the singing, teaching or small group times. Allow five to ten minutes for each testimony.

After the testimonies have finished, lead your group in five to six slow praise songs. Then begin your teaching with a review of last night's session:
> We know God wants to be worshipped.
> We know how we think of him affects our entire life.
> We know he doesn't change.
> We know that the more we know about him, the better our worship will be towards him.

After your review, move on to the next aspect of God you want to focus on:
> *God is omnipotent.* In the book of Job (particularly in chapters 22 and 27), the word "Almighty" is used fifty-six times. When people say "God almighty," I say, "Why yes, he is!" *Almighty* is reserved for God. Never in Scripture is it used in any other way. Almighty means "All-Powerful."

Next, look up Psalm 115:3 and read it together. Say, "People ask why God does or doesn't do certain things. The answer, according to Psalm 115, is he wants to. Period. He can do anything he wants."

Then ask, "What does this mean to you?"
1. Rest easy. He is in control. He's got the power.

2. Go to him in your need (read Hebrews 4:16). He can help.

3. Respect his power, just as you would a lion or a bear.

Then ask, "What does the Bible say about God's power?"
1. He can create something out of nothing (read Psalm 33:6; Romans 4:17; and Isaiah 44:24).

2. He sustains his creation (read Hebrews 1:3). Why do the atoms in this table stay in place? Because they're in a force in the universe (namely God) that holds it all in place.

3. He is able to save people from hell. Think of salvation, of what Jesus had to do. He faced:
   Opposition from the Jews
   The Devil and his schemes
   The requirements of the Law
   The spectre of death
   The weight of our sin
   The terror of the cross
   The terror of hell

4. He raised people from the dead (read John 5:28-29).

Then ask, "What's it all mean? So what?"

When we understand God's power, then our response is: Worship!

Now have individual students read the following verses:
   2 Kings 17:36
   Ephesians 3:20
   Psalms 121:1-2
   1 John 4:4
   Romans 8:33-35

Close with, "The bottom line is this: God's power is awesome. He deserves worship. He's got the power."

Next, give each student a 3-by-5 card. Play soft background music on tape to help set the tone. Give them about five minutes to write down anything that is worrying or troubling them on their card, then throw it in the metal trash can you have set next to you. Once all of the students have dropped their cards into the bin, light it on fire. Tell your kids that giving their worries and troubles over to God, the consuming fire, will reduce those concerns to ashes!

Close your time with a song of anthem like, "The Battle Belongs to the Lord."

11:20 a.m.-12:00 p.m. Four-Way Volleyball
Set up four volleyball nets in a big X so that you have space for four teams. Add four large inflatable beach balls and play a four-way volleyball game. The idea is to give up the least amount of points over a set time. If a ball touches the ground in a team's area, it's a point. Have judges posted at the four points and one in the

middle. Play for thirty minutes and award the winning team first in line for lunch.

1:00-5:30 p.m. Recreation time
        Activities you can offer to your students can include:
                Softball
                Volleyball
                Swimming
                Hiking (with an adult)
                Biking (rent bikes)
                Health club (if applicable)
                Football
                Horseback riding (cost involved)
                Mini golf
                Theater
                Nap
                Homework
                One-on-one time with adult leader

7:00-9:00 p.m. Session #3: Real Worship III
        Start with some fast singing. This is also a good time to have kids in your group share a solo song if they are musically gifted.

        After singing, play a crowd-breaking game such as "Pictionary," "Bible Pictionary," "Taboo," or "Guesstures." Follow your crowd breaker with more fast singing, then transition into student testimonies. Have two or three willing students share how God has been working in them so far this weekend.

        After your testimonies, spend about a half hour in praise and worship, singing slower praise songs that can help to usher you into the presence of God (see previous song suggestions). Then, begin your teaching.

        Begin by asking, "What physical position seems most natural when we think of worship?"

        Flat on our faces. Why? Because God is awesome. We know:
            that God wants us to worship him.
            that God is unchanging.
            that God is all-powerful.
            that God can help us with any of our needs.

        Then say, "Tonight, I want to focus on the importance of getting to know God deeply. What is worship? Worship is the adoration of God—vocally, physically, and visibly. We can worship God because he has made himself known to us—through the starry skies, the rising of the tide, the huge oceans, seeds that sprout, nature in its complexity, the wind, weather, currents and jet streams! We have to work at disbelieving that there is a God. It's natural to think there must be more to life than living and dying!"

Then say, "There are four by-products of getting to know God deeply. First, knowing God gives us the desire to be like him (read Jeremiah 9:24). Children often grow up to be like their fathers. So do Christians—we grow up spiritually according to our views of our Father in heaven."

Ask, "What is your view of our heavenly Father:
     Santa Claus?
     A surfer dude, without a care in the world?
     An old man in a chair waiting for time to go by?
     An awesome, loving, just God? To be respected and adored?"

Then say, "The more you know him the more you'll want to be like him. I find him good . . . I want to be better than I am. I find him strong . . . I want to be more confident. I find him to be in control . . . I am controlled.

"Second, knowing God reveals the truth about ourselves" (read Isaiah 6:1-2). Ask your students to suggest one word that describes what it would be like to be in front of God right now. After they've offered suggestions, have them look up Isaiah 6:5 together. Point out that getting too close to God shows us our cracks; we tend to avoid looking in a mirror like that! Be honest here and reveal a struggle of your own. Don't lay out a major moral failure, but let them know you are not perfect either.

Briefly review what you've covered so far, then say, "Third, knowing God helps us to see our world as it really is" (read Daniel 4:34-36). (Make this a quick point.)

Then say, "Fourth, knowing God helps us to realize that we will never arrive! We're always growing spiritually. Matthew 5:6 tells us that righteous are those that are hungry and thirsty. Ephesians 5:18 literally means that we are to be filled with the Holy Spirit over and over; we never arrive."

Close with, "The bottom line is this: Life's major goal is not knowing ourselves, but knowing God."

If you feel that it is appropriate, take the opportunity to invite students to respond to what they're learning about God by coming forward. Use your own style here. Invite the kids to come forward for salvation or some other specific commitment (to pray, study God's Word, witness, etc.). Have your staff prepared to follow up with responding students, while you close with three to four worship songs.

9:20-10:00 p.m. Sharing

Put a stool on the stage, platform, or just up front. Invite students to come up, sit on the stool, and share anything they want—what they've learned the most this weekend, a prayer need, a thank-you to someone special, a problem, or whatever. It can be a little hard at first; it is usually good to start yourself to set the tone, and prearrange with two to three willing students to share something. Warning: Once this gets going, it can get really emotional and eat up a lot of time. Don't be afraid to jump in and close this time when it's appropriate.

10:00-11:00 p.m. Free time

Have plenty of refreshments and board games on hand. Have student leaders head up the games.

11:00-11:45 p.m. Small groups

Have the students return to their rooms for small group time. Have their room leader ask each student to share one fun thing from the day, one meaningful thing, and one fact about God they learned today.

SUNDAY

8:00-8:30 a.m. Optional seminar: Who am I in Christ?

Follow the same format as the Saturday morning seminar. Ask the students how the following statements strengthen and encourage them:

> 2 Corinthians 5:17 (We are a new creation)
> Romans 8:1 (We are forgiven)
> Romans 8:16-17 (We are children of God and co-heirs with Christ)
> Romans 8:37 (We are more than conquerors)
> Colossians 3:3-4 (We are hidden in him)

When finished, have each student select one of the above to meditate on during the day.

9:15-10:00 a.m. Quiet time

Have the students read Psalm 1, then rewrite it in their own words.

10:00-10:45 a.m. Worship and communion

Sing a few worship songs to help the group focus on the Lord. Have the communion elements on tables in the four corners of the room. Instruct the students to get up and get the elements, take them back to their seat and quietly take communion either alone or with a friend. They should focus on God and his awesome power and forgiveness. They should confess any sins that they need to and take communion on their own when they feel ready. [**Note:** Feel free to adjust this communion time to fit the theology and traditions of your group.]

11:00 a.m.-12:00 p.m. Italian Softball

Italian softball is like regular softball, but you use a volleyball instead of a softball, and there are only two bases, home and first. As many people as can fit can be on base at one time, and players are tagged out by being hit with the ball. Each team gets three outs. Play as many innings as you like in the hour time frame. [**Editor's Note:** Since Becchetti is the publisher of this book, I decided to be politically incorrect to his ethnic group!]

1:30-2:00 p.m. Group photo and circle of prayer

After you take you group photo, have all of the students gather together in a circle. Ask three students to lead in a closing prayer.

Great Retreats for Youth Groups

WHEN I WAS YOUR AGE

Chris Cannon

THE BIG IDEA

This retreat is designed to:
- Build community and cohesiveness among volunteer and paid staff
- Train staff to understand the mind of today's adolescent
- Instill a passion and vision for effective relational ministry in your staff
- Enhance ownership within your staff of the ministry for the upcoming year
- Develop a sense of teamwork among the staff

WHO SHOULD ATTEND

All high school and/or junior high adult staff.

LOCATION

A cabin or retreat center that is large enough to accommodate your team.

TIME FRAME

Friday night through Sunday afternoon

WHAT TO BRING

✓ Sleeping bag
✓ Toiletries
✓ Bible
✓ Notebook
✓ Pen or pencil
✓ High school yearbook
✓ Whiteboard or easel with markers
✓ Extra spending money

NECESSARY INGREDIENTS

★ Meals (two breakfasts, one lunch, one dinner)
★ Yearbooks (Each leader brings his or her yearbook)
★ Copies of the *Leader's Survey* (found on page 157) for every participant
★ Video: *Molder of Dreams* (Focus on the Family)
★ TV monitor and VCR
★ Snacks
★ Camera

SCHEDULE

FRIDAY

8:00 p.m.	Arrive at cabin/ unpack/settle in
9:00 p.m.	Icebreakers
10:00 p.m.	Video: *Molder of Dreams*
11:30 p.m.	Reflection
12:30 a.m.	Lights out

SATURDAY

7:30 a.m.	Wake up
8:00 a.m.	Breakfast
9:00 a.m.	Quiet time
9:30 a.m.	Session #1: Rebuilding the Walls
11:00 a.m.	Concert of prayer
11:30 a.m.	Break
12:30 p.m.	Lunch
1:30 p.m.	Group activity
4:00 p.m.	Down time
6:00 p.m.	Dinner
7:30 p.m.	Praise and worship
8:00 p.m.	Session #2: Understanding Today's Teenager
9:30 p.m.	Concert of prayer
10:00 p.m.	Free time and games
12:00 a.m.	Lights out

SUNDAY

7:30 a.m.	Wake up
8:00 a.m.	Breakfast
9:00 a.m.	Quiet time
9:30 a.m.	Session #3: Keeping Your Well Full—Living the Balanced Life
11:00 a.m.	Pack and clean up
12:00 p.m.	Lunch
1:00 p.m.	Group prayer, hug, team picture
1:15 p.m.	Depart for home (lunch on the road as a group)

RETREAT COMPONENTS

FRIDAY

9:00-10:00 p.m. Icebreakers: *Two Truths and One Lie* and *Pass the Yearbook*

Two Truths and One Lie: Each leader is to state three things about himself or herself that were "true" during his or her high school years, two of which are actually true, and one a lie. The group tries to guess which of the three statements is a lie.

Pass the Yearbook: Each leader brings one of his or her high school yearbooks to the retreat. Pass the yearbooks around. It's a lot of fun to see each others' pictures and to read what everyone's high school friends wrote in the back of the books.

10:00-11:30 p.m. Video

Show the video *Molder of Dreams* with Guy Doud (available through Focus on the Family). This inspiring movie will help motivate your leadership to see the potential in kids who do not believe in themselves. Guy Doud is a "feeler" who will help your team rise to the challenge of "feeling" with kids through their difficult teen years.

Have snacks (popcorn, pretzels, sodas, etc.), paper, and pens available during this movie. It's packed with things your leaders will never want to forget (and don't forget the tissues!).

11:30 p.m.-12:00 a.m. Reflection

Spend some time reflecting on what was taught through the video. Ask questions like:

"What touched you the most?"

"What can you apply in your life as a 'Molder of Dreams'?"

"Who was the Guy Doud in your life?"

7:30 a.m. Wake up

Make sure you have plenty of coffee ready. Most likely your leadership team has been up all night talking and playing games together.

9:00-9:30 a.m. Quiet time

Send everyone out of the cabin or retreat site for their quiet time. Have them read the first two chapters of Nehemiah and Psalm 144. If they finish early, encourage them to take the remaining time to be silent and meditate on what they have just read.

9:30-11:00 a.m. Session #1: Rebuilding the Walls

Begin this time by asking some questions related to the book of Nehemiah, such as:

> "What is Nehemiah's response in chapter one to the condition of his people?"

> "Why do you think God used Nehemiah, as opposed to someone else? What made him different or special?"

> "What could the broken down walls symbolize in the lives of the kids we work with?" (e.g., divorce, the decline of public school education, unemployment, etc.—list all of the answers on a whiteboard)

> "What are the effects of what we have listed on the lives of our young people?" (e.g., gang activity, apathy, hopelessness, etc.—again, list these answers on the board)

Read Nehemiah 2:17-18 aloud to your staff. Ask them if they will join you in rebuilding the walls in the lives of the kids in your youth group.

Next, break everyone into groups of three. Ask them to identify, in their groups, one or two significant adults from their teen years. After everyone has completed this part, ask them to explain to one another why those people played such an important role in their lives and to list the qualities that they exemplified.

When everyone has completed both parts, bring the group back together and allow for sharing about the questions. Listen for common denominators, and comment on them as they arise, such as: "I've heard several of you mention a teacher who played an important role in your lives. What makes those teachers different from the rest you had in your life? Many of you have commented that the adult you mentioned was someone who believed in you. That's interesting, let's hang onto that thought. We'll discuss it later."

When the sharing is finished (keep it to around ten minutes), move into a teaching on the qualities you believe make great youth leaders. A good opening might be, "I'd like to share with you some thoughts about what makes a great youth worker. In my experience as a youth pastor, the following ingredients seem to be common threads among those who have been successful with kids and their families: "

A great youth worker spends time (see John 3:22).
A successful leader spends time with kids outside of church and scheduled events. Some creative ways to spend time with your kids can include:
> Washing you car together
> Grocery shopping
> Going out to eat
> Watching a sporting event
> Going to the mall

There are many ways to get together with kids that don't require extra time. Things that you might normally do could easily include a "disciple" for that time. You *don't* need to entertain them—they just want to be with you.

> Reflection Question: "Where do you see in your schedule an opening that you could use to spend time with a student in your group?"

A great youth worker affirms (see Hebrews 10:24-25).
Young people are constantly struggling with developing a proper, godly self-image. We are not just to give kids compliments and strokes, but to assist them in finding their identity in Christ. We are to train our kids to be God-pleasers. When we affirm kids, we represent the unmerited favor of God to kids in a real, physical manner.

> Reflection Question: "What can you do to build up the kids you're involved with that will not only encourage them, but also strengthen their walk with Christ?"

A great youth worker is honest (see Mark 10:17-22, particularly vs. 21).
How many of us want to be told if our zipper is down? Or if we have cheese hanging from our chin? Or if our lights are on? The answer is always yes, although we don't want to hear it! Just as Jesus told the rich young ruler the truth in love, so we too must tell kids the truth in love, even though it may hurt. These difficult areas

---

of discussion may involve dating, drug and alcohol use, music, or any number of hot topics. Kids *expect* us to tell them the truth biblically; we don't need to be afraid that we're going to surprise or shock them when we open our Bibles.

> Reflection Question: "Is there any situation or issue in the lives of any kids you're working with where you are reluctant to speak honestly and biblically to them? If so, why?"

A great youth worker inspires confidence (see Matthew 14:22-32).

According to psychologist H. Stephen Glenn, kids who have developed the belief that they can impact their world believe three things about themselves: they're capable, they're significant, and they're influential. Jesus communicated this to the apostles regularly, sending them out in twos to carry out his wondrous work. We need to allow our kids the chance to succeed *and* the chance to fail. They want a challenge, and often our confidence in them helps them rise to the occasion to meet that challenge.

> Reflection Question: "Who do you have a relationship with that could benefit from a dose of confidence building? How can you communicate your and God's confidence in him or her?"

A great youth worker is consistent (see Hebrews 13:8).

Many kids have, unfortunately, grown accustomed to changing standards of communication, living arrangements, friends, and significant adults. Yet we know that God is not like a man; he keeps his word. He's our sustainer, our rock, our fortress. Expecting and finding consistent responses and feedback from individual adults is very beneficial to kids' relationships with the Father. Our consistent responses and reactions to the daily victories and defeats our kids go through will develop their confidence in the Lord, who is "not a man, that he should change his mind" (Numbers 23:19; 1 Samuel 15:29).

> Reflection Question: "Is there anyone who you have been inconsistent with? If so, what can you do to strengthen your character and reconcile any damaged relationships?"

11:00-11:30 a.m. Concert of prayer

Break the group into twos and threes. Direct a time of prayer into specific areas. All of the groups can pray together at the same time. The idea is that at least a few people pray for each request. Subjects for prayer can include:
- Community
- Parents
- Local high schools

- Kids
- Other youth leaders

Encourage everyone to keep their prayers short to allow for more participation and to ensure that all of the topics can be covered in prayer.

1:30-4:00 p.m. Group activity

This is play time! Encourage everyone to do this together. Possible activities can include hiking, shopping, a team sport, or a game. Although you want to stress togetherness, allow your staff to do whatever they like during this time. Some will feel the need to rest or just be alone.

6:00-7:30 p.m. Dinner

If you are preparing your own meals for your retreat, it is good to involve everyone in one of the two roles of each meal (preparation and clean up). This again helps to strengthen the sense of unity and teamwork.

At dinner, have your leaders complete the Leader's Survey found on page 157.

7:30-8:00 p.m. Praise and Worship

Spend time singing praise songs and choruses like "More Love, More Power," "Spirit of the Living God," "Day by Day," "Alleluia," "Behold What Manner of Love," "Bind us Together," and "In His Name."

8:00-9:30 p.m. Session #2: Understanding Today's Teenager

Begin by having everyone share their answers to the *Leader's Survey*. There will undoubtedly be some great answers! Write some of the answers on the left-hand side of a whiteboard. When everyone has finished, brainstorm the answers a typical fifteen-year-old guy and girl might give, and put those responses on the right side.

This is a great jumping-off point for discussing the condition of young people today versus your generation. Good lead-in questions include, "What are some differences here? How do we explain these huge differences? Are teenagers different than we were, is society different, or neither? If you were a teenager today, how different do you think your life would have been?"

[**OPTION:** At this point, you may wish to use data regarding the "Buster Generation" from a book by George Barna called *The Invisible Generation: Baby Busters* (1992, Barna Research Group) to reinforce the contrasts between generations.]

When you have finished discussing the above questions, walk your staff through the needs that all teenagers have from generation to generation:

The need to be known. Everyone wants to be recognized and called by their first name. Taking time to learn names and phone numbers is a sincere form of flattery and affirmation.

The need to make a difference. Young people are driven to change their world. They have the energy and desire to make a difference. As Tony Campolo stated in his book *The Church and the American Teenager* (1989, Youth Specialties), "If this generation of teenagers is lost to the church, it will not be because we demanded too much from them, but because we demanded too little."

The need to belong. Adolescence is marked by the struggle to determine one's social and individual identity. Huge numbers of teenagers are joining gangs because they are able to find clearly defined standards of acceptance and approval that satisfy their need to belong. Creating and communicating group norms will assist this often informal process.

The need to be needed. We all want to be missed if we aren't able to attend a meeting or event; kids are no different. They want to be noticed if they are missing and welcomed when they return. A warm welcome can do much to communicate the value we attach to kids who attend our meetings. Cards and phone calls communicate that we esteem them regardless of their attendance.

The need for purpose. The above four needs are null and void without giving students a sense of purpose. That purpose, of course, is found in the redemptive work of Jesus Christ on the cross. Without the cross, our kids will save the whales, rescue the environment, and build orphanages to satisfy their own need for purpose. Yet the Great Commission (Matthew 28:18-20) lays a bold path of action, a course that offers our kids the challenge and mission that will truly satisfy their need for purpose.

Close this time by giving your staff the following reflection questions:
- Whose name do I need to memorize? What else can I do to let these kids know that they are known and valuable to me?
- What can I do to help kids make a difference? Are there any needs in the church or the community they could meet?
- What practical steps can I take to help kids feel that they belong to our youth group?
- How can I demonstrate more effectively that the kids I minister to are significant regardless of their attendance at youth group? How can I let them know I care about them, and care whether they are walking with

the Lord or not?

- Are there any students that I have failed to challenge and exhort to reach their potential in Christ? Have I been reluctant to honestly present Christ to anyone in our youth group, thereby failing to help that person find his or her purpose in Christ?

9:30-10:00 p.m. Concert of prayer

Break your group into twos and threes. Direct them into a time of prayer where they pray specifically, by name, for the kids that God has laid on their hearts to reach out to for Christ.

SUNDAY

9:00-9:30 a.m. Quiet time

Have your leaders read Mark 6:14-56 (A Day in the Life of Jesus). Encourage them to take time to pray and meditate on the things they have learned over the weekend and the things that they have committed themselves to do. Ask them to pray for the students that they are discipling.

9:30-10:45 a.m. Session #3: Keeping Your Well Full—Living the Balanced Life

Begin this time by affirming your staff for all the hard work they do, the relationships they nurture, and the support they provide you. Acknowledge the sacrifices they make by going to football games, lock-ins, and retreats.

Ask a few questions at this point like, "What has been a special highlight for you in ministry over the past several months? What are you looking forward to seeing God do in the next several months?"

These questions provide a lead-in for a discussion about personal time management. Begin by reading 1 Thessalonians 2:8-9, drawing attention to the time commitment involved in relational youth ministry inferred in these passages.

Next, begin a brainstorming time by asking, "What does the balanced, stable life include or look like? What are the essential components?" (For instance, solitude, working out, quiet time, etc.)

Record these answers on a whiteboard where everyone can see them. Allow five to eight minutes for sharing. When this is completed, have your staff split up into twos and threes. Then say, "Look over your week-at-a-glance schedules. What changes, if any, do you or your partners think you might need to make to develop a more stable life? Take about ten minutes to share, then pray for one another."

When everyone has finished sharing and praying, begin your teaching by reading Mark 1:32-35 and Matthew 14:13-23. Ask the following questions:
> "What can we learn about the demands of ministry from these
>   passages?"
> "What did Jesus model for us in these passages?"
> "How do *you* handle the stress from ministry?"

Now walk your staff through the components of the stable life:

Regular devotions. If they were good enough for Jesus, they are good enough for us. Show your group how to use the acronym P.R.A.Y.: Praise, Repent, Ask, Yield.

Family time. We can't neglect our families to save someone else's family. God can send someone else to the needy kids in our youth group, but we are responsible for our own family.

Peer fellowship. High schoolers can't be our only friends. Involvement in home fellowships or discipleship or accountability with people our own ages is a must.

Exercise. Exercising and working out may seem optional, but if ignored, they'll remind us of the need to take care of our temples. When possible, we should find workout partners with whom we can fellowship.

Conclude this time with more affirmation and exhortation. Close with a prayer of blessing upon your staff. Say something like, "Giving your very life, as Paul puts it in 1 Thessalonians 2:8, requires commitment and time. But always allow for your own well to be filled by living a stable, balanced life. Jesus promised us living water; let's commit ourselves to these priorities so that our wells won't run dry, leaving us with nothing to offer our family, friends, or students in ministry. Let me conclude by praying for us . . . "

1:00-1:15 p.m. Group prayer, hug, team picture

Have your group form a hand-held circle. Have each staff member pray for the person on the right, commissioning that person to service as a leader in the youth ministry.

When you've completed your prayer, have a group hug, then keep everyone together for a team picture.

Leader's Survey

1. What was the first album or tape you bought? (Any eight tracks?)

2. Who was your favorite rock band or musician?

3. Who did you have a crush on as a teenager?

4. Who were your heroes or role models?

5. What was your favorite television show?

Great Retreats for Youth Groups

SECTION THREE

RESOURCES

HOW TO PREPARE A GREAT RETREAT

Mike DeVito and Kara Eckmann

WAY EARLY
Choose campground or location
Choose date
Choose theme/purpose
Choose speaker
Choose worship/music leader
Verify budget

EIGHT WEEKS IN ADVANCE
Determine cost, registration deadline, departure, and arrival times, arrange for transportation (buses, van to leave early)

SIX WEEKS IN ADVANCE
Begin promotion
Flyers/mailers (include camp phone numbers, "What to Bring" lists, and permission slip)
Skits
Posters
Videos from past retreats
"Top Ten Reasons to Go on the Retreat" (break from homework, parents, new friends, food, God)
Find registration person
Get input from staff—teaching theme
Find recreation time

FOUR WEEKS IN ADVANCE
Think about theme song(s)
Give graphics person needed posters for retreat
Contact speaker if necessary
Contact music/worship leader if necessary
Have staff call and invite students

THREE WEEKS IN ADVANCE
Create camp posters
Registration poster
Posters for inside and outside of dorms (sign for girls and guys with arrows for inside dorm)

Posters for dining halls
Posters for meeting hall
Posters for each team
Communicate with staff re: special clothes, props to bring
Prepare staff with small-group leading skills
Set goals and expectations for the retreat with the staff
Find staff member to make food baskets for speaker and music person and arrange for baskets to be brought to retreat site in the van early
Find sound person
Determine who should leave for camp early to set up sound and decorate the camp
Turn in check requests for speaker, musician, and bus

TWO WEEKS IN ADVANCE

Finalize retreat schedule
Send speaker and musician copy of schedule
Brainstorm meal ideas (luau, western, formal, 50s, picnic, tie hands together, victory celebration, breakfast in bed/in dorm hall, breakfast outside, progressive, pep rally)
Brainstorm ways to decorate dorms and bathrooms
Find staff member to video
Find staff and students to help in registration
Ask staff who they want in their rooms
Find someone to supervise any Sunday or Wednesday church services that we will miss (maybe find a video)

ONE WEEK IN ADVANCE

Buy:
> Bedtime snacks
> Food for special treats
> Balloons for registration
> Materials to decorate dorm and dining hall (balloons, streamers, coolers for food, etc.)

Photocopy:
> Encouragement letters
> Bed signs
> Signs for room doors
> Signs to have on meal tables
> Signs for bathrooms
> Room lists
> Camp schedule

Obtain special music and decorations for meals
Talk to maintenance people re: needed equipment
Write directions for group going to camp early
> Include map to camp

Include map of dorm and meeting hall with poster locations
Decide room lists
Team divisions (if applicable)
Registration instructions
Type alphabetical gender list so easier to locate
Find staff and students to distribute encouragement letters
Decide prize for camp winner (e.g., free snack at snack bar)
Call fast-food restaurant to notify that bus will be stopping
Obtain any necessary videos
Leave schedule and announcements for church services we'll miss

DAY OF THE RETREAT

Get needed supplies and sound equipment
Registration—set up table, balloons, posters
Ink our pens

ONE WEEK AFTER RETREAT

Write thank-you notes to speaker and musician
Write letter of appreciation to staff
Evaluate retreat

TWO WEEKS AFTER RETREAT

Plan a "flashback" event with kids and parents—include testimonies, present awards (serious and silly), and show video or slide presentation

SAMPLE PERMISSION SLIP

Included is an example of an excellent permission slip. Before adapting any form, have your church leadership review it, and consult a local attorney for input. No permission slip, no matter how well done, is an absolute safeguard against possible liability. It is, however, a reflection to parents about the seriousness of your ministry and your commitment to care for their kids.

Keep all permission slips together in a three-ring binder on the trip. Have a place for both parents, if necessary, to include their work phone numbers and other important information such as FAX numbers, beeper numbers, and cellular phone numbers. You want to be able to reach parents as quickly as possible if a situation arises that requires their attention.

These permission slips also serve as a great reference for you and your staff. All of the information included in the permission slip is helpful to you on a regular basis. Save these completed forms, making copies for your volunteer staff and yourself. [**Note:** A completed permission slip is always required for each trip, with the slip indicating which trip the parents are giving approval for their child to attend. Honor your church, parents, and kids with excellence in your permission slip.]

PARENT PERMISSION - RELEASE FORM

Event name _____ Event Dates_____

Name _____Birthdate _____

Social Security # _____Core Group Leader _____

Address _____High School _____

Home Phone (_____)_____ Work Phone(_____)_____

Year of Graduation From High School_____

Authorization of Consent to Treatment of Minor:
(I) (We), the undersigned, parent(s) of _____a minor, do hereby authorize _____, youth ministry leaders, as agent(s) for the undersigned to consent to any x-ray examination, anesthetic, medical or surgical diagnosis or treatment, and hospital care which is deemed advisable by, and is to be rendered under the general or specific supervision of any physician and surgeon licensed under the provision of the Medical Practice Act, whether such diagnosis or treatment is rendered at the office of said physician or at a hospital.

It is understood that this authorization is given in advance of any specific diagnosis, treatment, or hospital care being required, but is given to provide authority and power on the part of our aforesaid agent(s) to give specific consent to any and all such diagnosis, treatment, or hospital care which the aforementioned physician in the exercise of his best judgement may deem advisable.

This authorization is given pursuant to the provisions of _____ (your state's civil code number) of the Civil Code of _____ (your state). This authorization shall remain effective through the above named minor's graduation from high school, unless sooner revoked in writing delivered to said agent(s).

Release of_____(church name):
_____(Parent's name) shall indemnify, hold free and harmless, assume liability for, and defend_____(church name), its agents, servants, employees, officers, and directors from any and all costs and expenses including but not limited to, attorney's fees, reasonable investigative and discovery costs, court costs, and all other sums which _____ (church name), assertion of liability, or any claim or action founded thereon, arising or alleged to have arisen out of _____ (child's name) use of real or personal property belonging to _____ (church name), its' agents, servants, employees, officers, and directors, or by action of omission by _____ (child's name).

Parent _____ (signature)

Parent _____ (signature)

Home Phone _____ Work Phone _____

Other phone numbers_____ Phone _____

Legal Guardian_____ Phone _____

Other Emergency Contact_____ Phone _____

Family Doctor_____ Phone _____

Insurance Co._____ If None Please Check ____

Insurance Policy # or Group # _____

Known Medical Conditions_____

_____

_____

Medications? _____

_____

_____

Allergies? _____

_____

_____

Last Tetanus Immunization?_____

Will You Allow Blood Transfusions? _____   _____ Initials of parent

_____ Initials of parent

Contact Lenses? _____

Other _____

_____

_____

_____

_____

_____

RETREAT CHECKLIST

SUPPLIES
—— Extra Bibles
—— Name tags
—— Lesson plans, handouts
—— Cameras/film/video
—— Song sheets, musical instruments
—— Audio-visual equipment
—— Equipment for games and activities

RETREAT SITE
—— Maps and clear, correct directions
—— Telephone number of site left at church office

FOOD
—— Snacks
—— Meals
—— Beverages
—— Special food for those with dietary needs

VEHICLES
—— Full tank of gas
—— Registration and insurance documents
—— Check of traffic and road conditions

EMERGENCIES
—— First aid kit
—— Name, address, and directions to nearest hospital

DOCUMENTS
—— Money collected and safely stored (never take the money with you)
—— Petty cash
—— Completed permission slips for every student and adult volunteer
—— Retreat evaluations
—— Room assignment sheet
—— Retreat rules

Great Retreats for Youth Groups

Mike DeVito and Kara Eckmann

More than anything else, the success of a retreat is dependent upon the atmosphere that is created before, during, and after the actual weekend. The following ideas will enhance any retreat and can be adapted to fit virtually any theme and size of group.

RETREAT PROMOTION AND PREPARATION

Promotion

Flyers distributed in church and mailed to students' homes

Separate letter to parents

Visit the camp and make a promotional video

Posters in creative locations such as bathroom stalls and on bathroom mirrors

Church bulletin announcements

A list of "Top Ten Reasons to Go to Camp" or "Top Ten Reasons Not to Go to Camp"

Drama sketches

Preparation

Make a timeline to help you work backwards from the actual retreat date

Secure the location of your retreat considering factors such as distance, weather and recreation opportunities

Determine how much to charge each student based on price of camp facility, speaker, worship leader, transportation, program and adult staff needs (you may want to charge your students more so you can offer your adult staff a discount)

Pick a theme that fits with the unique needs of your youth ministry at that time

Choose a speaker and/or worship leader that fits with your theme

Determine transportation needs

Secure a volunteer to be in charge of registration (this will relieve stress!)

Emphasize the importance of students bringing medical releases with current medical insurance information

Meet with your volunteer adult leaders to pray, discuss vision, and ask your adults to submit a list of students they would like to room with at the camp

If you are stopping at a fast-food restaurant on the way to camp or on the way home, call the restaurant beforehand so they can be ready for you

THE ATMOSPHERE AS YOU LOAD THE VEHICLES

Meet with your adult volunteers thirty minutes early to pray

Ask adult staff and student leaders to greet arriving students

Assign staff to load the luggage

Hang a large welcome sign with helium balloons

Have rowdy music playing

Who students room with is crucial to them—make a preliminary room list in advance, but be open to changes as you watch who comes with whom and who sits with whom on the bus

Have a quick meeting with the students to:

Welcome them to the retreat

Introduce guests

Explain briefly what the retreat will be like so they feel comfortable (don't say too much so they will still be surprised!)

Assign leaders to promote on-the-way fun and games

THE ATMOSPHERE ON THE ROAD

[**Note:** You are too preoccupied to do this! Your staff ratio for the retreat should be one adult for every four kids.]

If your van or bus has the capabilities, play Christian music videos or appropriate movies

Try some games on the road

- Body scavenger hunt (i.e. "I need a driver's license")
- Tape trivia questions under car or bus seats

THE ATMOSPHERE UPON ARRIVAL AT THE RETREAT

Posters for the camp driveway—the first poster can say something like "Get Ready," the second poster can say "Get Set," and the third poster can say "Go For It!"

Plaster posters with your theme on every possible outside wall

Helium balloons

Volunteer adults to help carry their luggage to their rooms

Signs on each room door welcoming them

On each bed, place welcome sign and a few candies

Put a cooler in each room stocked with sodas and frozen Snickers (restock as needed)

THE ATMOSPHERE DURING SERVICES

Have a hot opener

Choose a rowdy theme song that you will play right before each meeting

Include an ongoing skit—each meeting, add a new development to the skit

Have a "Word of the Day"—whenever the speaker or camp director say a certain word (i.e. toilet paper), everyone must fall to the floor

Have lyrics for ALL songs—nothing will ruin worship like not knowing the words to the songs

Set up a small table with a shoe box labeled "Encouragement Box"—put some pencils and stationery next to the box and let students write "encouragement notes" to each other all weekend (keep the box going when you get back to church)

Video the day's events and play a highlight video each evening

Put up pieces of paper in each bathroom with the same question (e.g., "What's the biggest lie you have ever told?"). Ask students to write their anonymous responses. Read their responses during your meetings. You won't believe the creativity!

Devote one meeting to helping students put their faith in action by helping clean the camp or doing a service project nearby

THE ATMOSPHERE DURING MEALS

To accentuate the theme:
>   Posters
>   Music
>   Dressing up
>   Playing videos
>   Changing the lighting
>   Add crowd breakers to meal times
>   Serve food that correlates with theme

For each theme meal you can either let your students know ahead of time so they can bring specific clothing, or just ask adults to dress up, or encourage students to be creative in finding appropriate clothes for specific theme meals using what they have brought

Each meal a different decade (the 1950's—Sock Hop, Happy Days look; the 1960's—Hippie, Flower Child; the 1970's—Disco)

Hawaiian Luau—serve Hawaiian punch, pineapple

Country Western B.B.Q.—Great if outside and can sit on hay

Beach Bonfire—Beach Boys music, surfboard props

Breakfast in Bed—Bring students breakfast in bed, playing obnoxious wake-up music or more sophisticated classical music

Picnic—Spread out blankets and chow on the floor

Candlelight dinner—Staff dress up and serve the students—dim the lights, light candles, play classical music

Pajama party—Students come to breakfast in their pajamas (play theme music from cartoons to complete the mood)

Outdoor tailgater—Put on marching band music and have your own pep rally outside (best in the snow!)

THE ATMOSPHERE DURING RECREATION

A well thought-out, prepared, and creative program is a must

Give more team points for attitude and cooperation than ability and victories

Think about a recreation theme (i.e., winter sports, Super Bowl, cartoons, Olympics)

THE ATMOSPHERE FOR COUNSELORS

Ask counselors how they are doing, share prayer requests (if your counselor group is large, distribute sheets and ask them to write how they are doing so that they can receive strategic prayer)

During free time, have a special hangout room for counselors where you give them soft drinks, chips, and cookies (they deserve it)

Provide ideas for how to follow up students when they return home

THE ATMOSPHERE DURING WORSHIP

Make sure you have song lyrics available (overhead transparencies work best because you don't have to worry about calling out song numbers or flipping through books)

Select a worship theme song that you sing often

THE ATMOSPHERE FOR YOUR SPEAKER AND WORSHIP LEADER

Place a special basket in their room that includes snacks and drinks, gum, and throat drops

Invite them to counselor meetings so they feel a part of the team

THE ATMOSPHERE AS YOU GO HOME

Put up posters for students to see on their way home from camp that reminds them of the theme

Spend time at your next youth service sharing highlights of the retreat and discussing how to persevere now that you're back home